Succeeding a

NATIONAL CURRICULUM
MATHS

Your guide to the KS2 National Curriculum Tests

Philip Power

Collins*Children's*Books
Copyright © HarperCollins Publishers Ltd 1997

Note for Pupils

What do the Key Stage 2 National Tests mean to you?

The tests help you check your progress in **English**, **Science** and **Mathematics** through Key Stage 2. By assessing your strengths and weaknesses they enable you to set your targets for future progress in these subjects. Your teachers will send the results of your test to your secondary school to help them decide the best subject group for you.

When will you take these tests?

They take place in May of each year.

What do the Maths National Tests consist of?

- ◆ The tests are divided into 2 main parts: Tests A and B. They are both of equal standard.
- ◆ Both tests will take 45 minutes each. You will be given 5 minutes to read the instructions beforehand.
- ◆ The tests set questions to see how well you understand the four main parts of the curriculum for Key Stage 2. These are: Number; Shape; Space and Measures and Handling Data.

What is a level?

While at school you will have the chance to progress through 8 levels in each subject. By the end of Key Stage 2 you should expect to be between levels 3 and 5. The results give the level you can expect to be placed in for each subject.

What does this book do for you?

- It shows the layout of the tests, and the types of questions you can expect.
- It shows you how to follow instructions precisely.
- It gives you practice in writing the test, and the confidence that comes with preparation.
- It shows you how to assess your own answers.

How to use this book

Get an adult to read through the instructions for each section with you, and to tell you when to start and finish the test. They should help you to assess your answers and determine your approximate level.

Top Tips

- Tackle each question. **No answer means no marks.**
- Remember always to show your working in the box where provided. You will get extra marks for correct working-out shown.
- **Don't panic.** If you practise in your weaker areas you'll be ready for the real test.
- With an adult use the boxes in the margin of the test papers to insert the marks you have awarded yourself. Write a total at the bottom of the page, and transfer the totals to page 48.

Equipment you will need

You will need the following equipment for answering the questions:

- a pen, pencil and rubber
- a ruler (30 cm plastic ruler is most suitable)
- a calculator (one with four functions is all you require)
- an angle-measurer
- tracing paper
- a mirror

You may **not** use a calculator in Test A.
You may use one in Test B.

Tests A and B

Instructions

1) Read the questions very carefully.

2) The questions for you to answer are in tinted boxes.

3) Look for the ✎ to show where you write the answer.

4) You **must** show your working if you are asked to do so but you are allowed to use the test paper for rough working whenever you need to.

5) If you can't do a question, leave it and return to it later.

6) You have 45 minutes for Test A and 45 minutes for Test B.

7) You may **not** use a calculator for Test A.

8) You may use a calculator for Test B.

Test A

1. A **pair** of numbers below adds up to more than 100.
Circle **the pair** of numbers.

2   27

54   45   36

48   21

2. **Three** of the numbers below add up to 42.
Circle the **three** numbers.

25   2

27   14   1

16   18

3. In the circle write **+**, **−**, **×** or **÷** to make the calculation correct.

7 × 6 ◯ 6 = 36

Test A

4 Mrs. Butler and Mrs. Cooper visit the bakers.
The special offers that day include:

One large apple pie
£1.80

Six small sponge cakes
£1.20

One granary loaf
85p

One French loaf
55p

Mrs. Butler has £2.00 in her purse.

a) Having bought one of the special offers, **she has exactly 20 pence left**.
What did she buy?

_____

Mrs. Cooper has five 20 pence pieces in her purse.
She buys a granary loaf.

b) How much **change** does she get?

Show your working.
You may get a mark.

pence

total

Test A

5 Paula's six friends received the following amounts of pocket money each week:

Name	Amount
Dave	£1.20
Shahied	£0.50
Mary	£0.75
Antonio	40p
Lee	£0.90
Sue	£1.00

a) How much **more** did Dave get **than** Antonio?   ⬚ pence

Here is a graph of how much each received, but Mary's is missing.

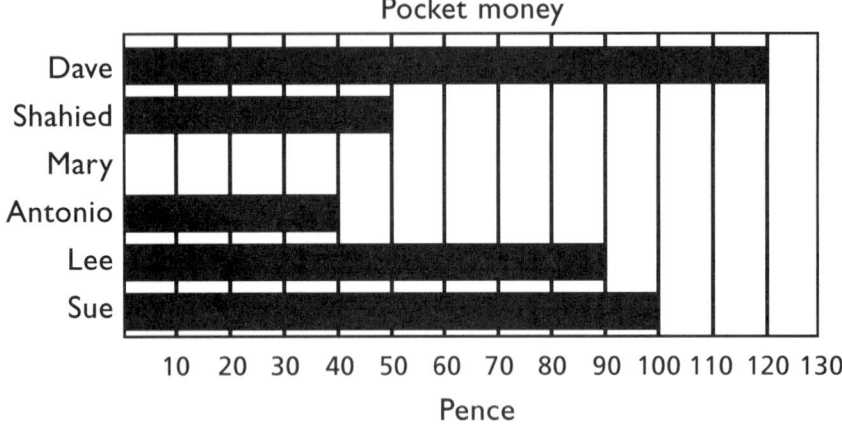

b) Draw a bar on the graph to show how much **Mary** received.

6 An isosceles triangle has two of its sides of equal length. One of the sides has been drawn on the grid.

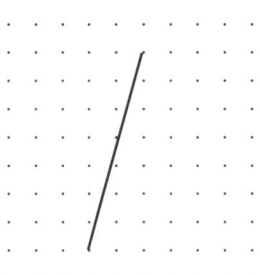

Use a ruler to draw two **more** lines **to complete** the isosceles triangle.

7 Write in the **missing** digit.

$$\begin{array}{r} 7\square \\ \times\ 6 \\ \hline 468 \end{array}$$

1

8 A new type of trainers comes with either Ordinary Grip soles or with Special Grip soles.

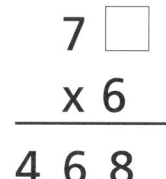

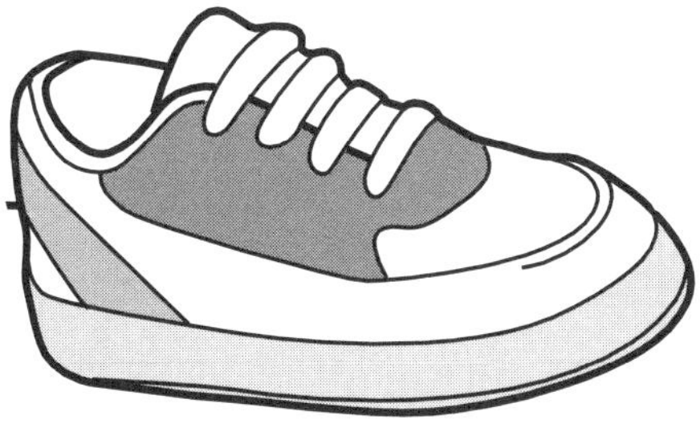

They are priced as follows:

	Ordinary Grip	Special Grip
Size 1	£17.50	£18.50
Size 2	£18.25	£19.75
Size 3	£19.00	£21.00
Size 4	£19.75	£22.25
Size 5	£20.50	£23.50
Size 6	£21.25	£24.75

An extra pair of laces costs £0.75.

John buys a pair of Size 5 Special Grip Trainers and an extra pair of laces.

a) How much does John spend? £

1

Gemma spends exactly £22.00 and includes a pair of laces in her purchase.

b) What trainers does she buy?

2

total

Test A

9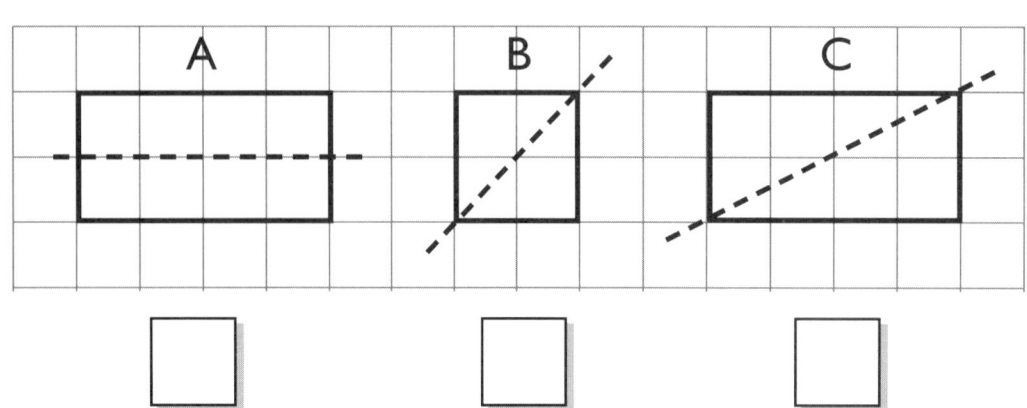

a) Put **ticks** in the boxes **if** the dotted lines in A, B and C **are lines of symmetry**.

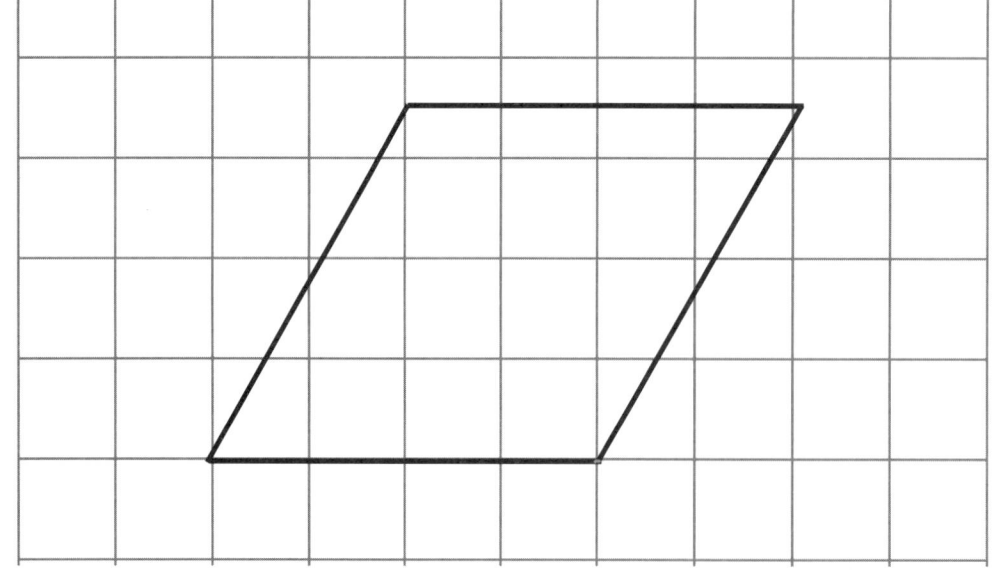

b) Draw two lines of symmetry on the shape above.

1

1

total

Test A

10 Near the end of a game of solitaire (**A**), four marbles are still left. The board is then moved through one right angle.

Draw how the board (**B**) looks **now**.
You may use tracing paper.

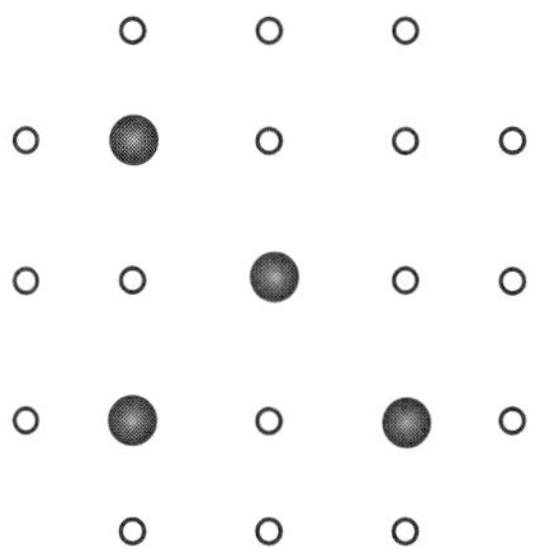

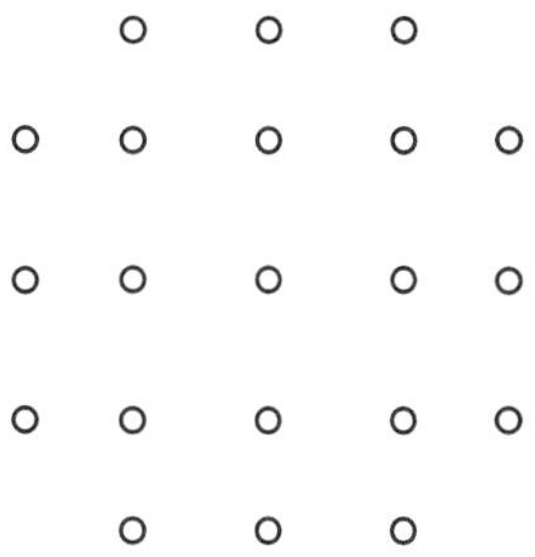

11   T = True   F = False

This triangle has   two or more equal sides [T]
                     one or more right angles [F]
                     two pairs of parallel sides [F]

Put **T** (True) or **F** (False) in the squares after the statements below

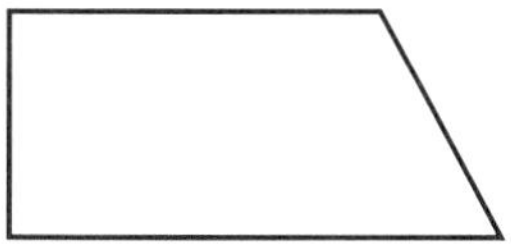

This trapezium has   two or more equal sides ☐
                      one or more right angles ☐
                      two pairs of parallel sides ☐

This square has   two or more equal sides ☐
                   one or more right angles ☐
                   two pairs of parallel sides ☐

12   Write in the **missing** numbers.

3 × 30 = ☐
☐ + 45 = 62
50 − ☐ = 34

total

9

Test A

13 Six children held a 'throw the tennis ball' competition.
The teacher measured the distances thrown:

Name	Distance
Tom	22.75m
Jane	17.60m
Sara	26.50m
Tim	18.15m
Nishma	14.20m
Bob	15.00m

a) How much further in centimetres was the longest throw than the shortest?

Show your working. You may get a mark.

2

The children then raced back to the classroom.
The teacher timed them as follows:

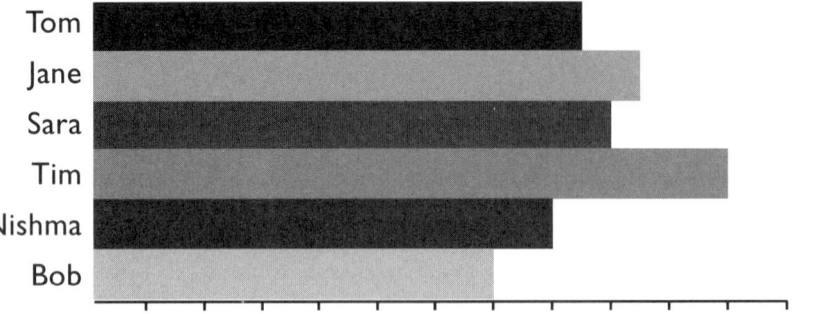

b) Who was the first one in the race back to the classroom?

1

total

10

14 David asks 50 different people to choose a card from his selection of six lettered cards.

| A | B | E | M | P | O |

Kirsty asks 50 different people to choose a card from her selection of ten lettered cards.

| A | C | E | F | J | N | I | O | S | U |

David believes that more of the 50 people will pick a letter 'A' from his selection than will pick a letter 'A' from Kirsty's selection.

a) Give **a** reason why **he** is correct.

David is correct because _____
_____
_____

A, E, I, O and U are vowels.

Kirsty believes that the first person to choose a card from her selection and from David's selection are equally likely to pick a vowel.

b) Give **a** reason why **Kirsty** is correct.

Kirsty is correct because _____
_____
_____

Test A

15 A gardener divides his garden into different sized plots of land on which he grows brussels sprouts plants.
The bigger the plot the more brussels sprouts plants he grows.

Area of plot	3m²	6m²	9m²	12m²	15m²
No. of brussels sprouts plants	8	14	20	26	32

For each plot, the number of plants grown is twice the area, add 2.

a) What would be the **area** of a plot which had **44** plants?

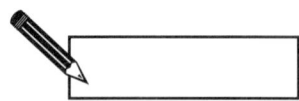

1

For each plot, the number of plants (P) is twice the area (A), add 2.

b) Write this in **symbols**.

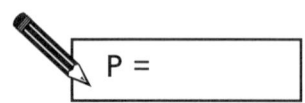 P =

2

c) What is the **perimeter** of the plot of land which has 32 plants, if **all four sides** are whole number lengths of, at least, 3 metres?

Show your working. You may get a mark.

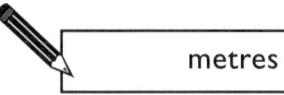 metres

2

total

12

Write in the **missing** digit.

☐16 ÷ 18 = 12

A village is trying to raise money for new equipment on the playground. A notice is put up on the village board to show how much progress has been made.

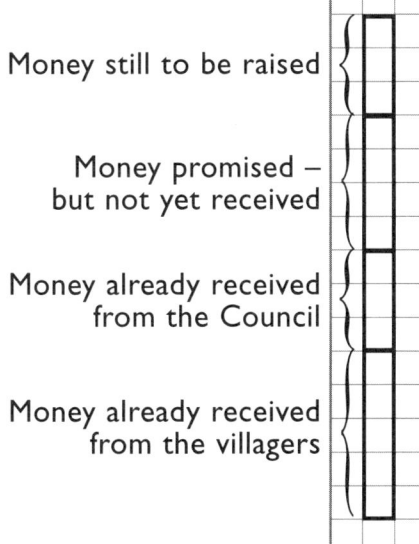

Money still to be raised

Money promised – but not yet received

Money already received from the Council

Money already received from the villagers

a) Do you **estimate** from the diagram, that more than 50% of the money needed has already been received?
Answer yes, **or** no.

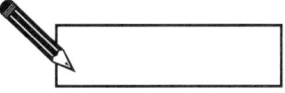

b) If £1800 is needed in total, **estimate** how much money still needs to be raised. **Use the diagram to help you.**

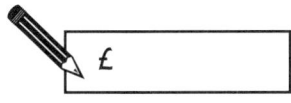

c) Of the £600 already received from the villagers, 25% came from **one** man. **How much** did he give?

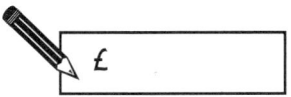

13

Test A

18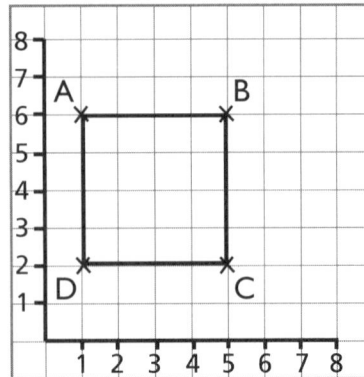

The four corners of a square have been plotted on the grid above. They are:
A (1,6), B (5,6), C (5,2) and D.

a) What are the **co-ordinates** of D?

1

b) **Plot** the **centre point** of the square.
Write down the co-ordinates of **this point**.

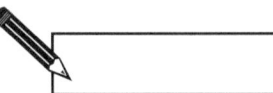

1

19 Angle A and angle B together make up a right angle (90°).

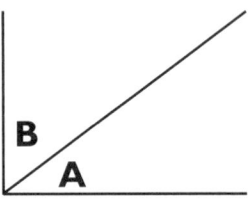

a) Use an angle measurer to find **the size of angle B**.

 °

1

b) Draw accurately the **next 4** centimetre straight line at right angles to the **2** centimetre line. You may use an angle measurer.

2

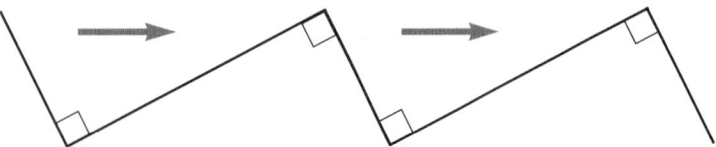

total

14

Test B

1   [7]   [1]   [4]

147 is the smallest number that can be made by arranging the three digits above.

a) What is the **largest** number that can be made by rearranging the three digits?

b) Using **all** the digits, write a number which is an **even** number.

2 John spends 87p at the shop. He gives the shopkeeper a £1 coin. He receives 3 coins as change.

What were the 3 coins?

15

Test B

3 The local sports centre organised a holiday activity course on five mornings during one week of the holidays. Each morning, the children took part in **one** activity of their choice.

	Swimming	Tennis	Cricket	Computing	Art
Monday	12	0	15	0	0
Tuesday	18	4	9	4	8
Wednesday	30	8	16	12	4
Thursday	23	12	0	12	10
Friday	25	4	8	6	12

a) How **many** children did computing on **Thursday**?

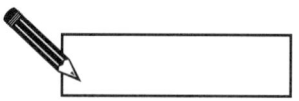

This is a graph showing the number of children doing one of the activities.

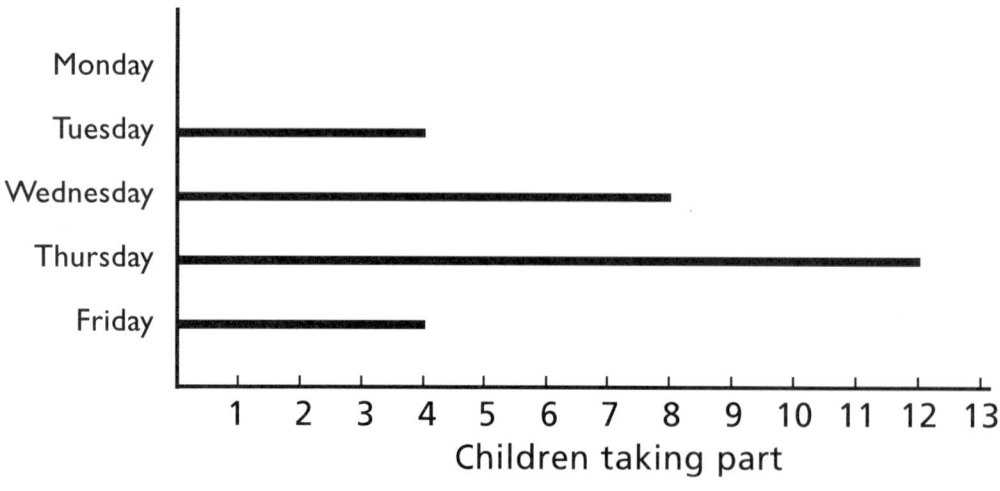

Children taking part

b) **Which** activity is it?

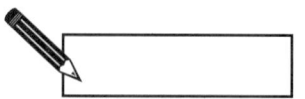

c) How many **more** do this activity on a Thursday than on a Friday?

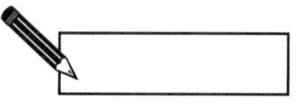

16

4 The teacher has written these numbers on the board. The pair of linked numbers has a difference of 9.

17   36   16
41   23   30   14
3   26   31

Write in the boxes below **the other pair of numbers** with a difference of 9.

5 Write in the boxes below the two numbers from those written on the board in question 4 which will divide by 4 with no remainder.

6 Write in the **missing** digits.

```
  □ 5 5
- 1 8 □
  3 7 4
```

7 A jar contains 260 sweets. They are shared equally among 10 children.

How many does **each** child get?

sweets

Test B

8 A block of chocolate comes in the shape of a triangular prism.

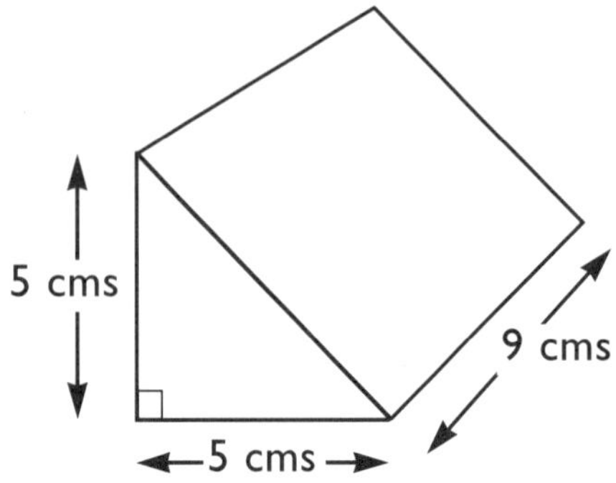

5 cms
9 cms
5 cms

What is the **area** of the triangular **face**?

Show your working. You may get a mark.

[2]

Which of these wrapping paper shapes are nets which would just cover the block of chocolate? Put a tick (✔) if it is a net that would cover the chocolate, put a (✘) if it is not.

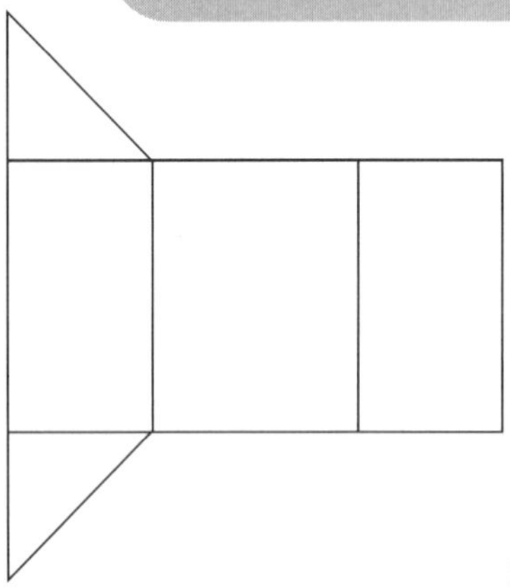

A

B

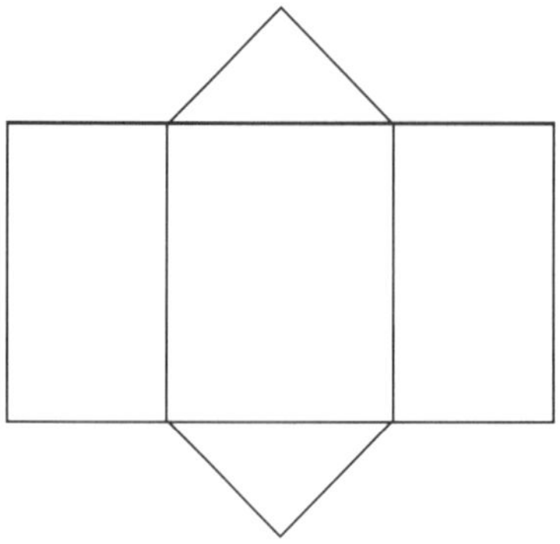

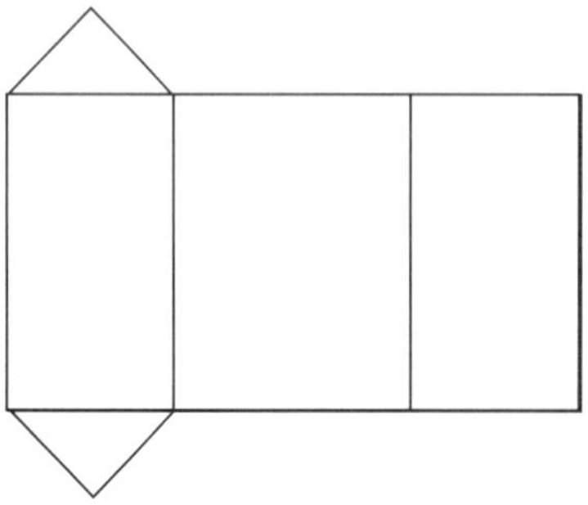

C

[2]

18

total

9

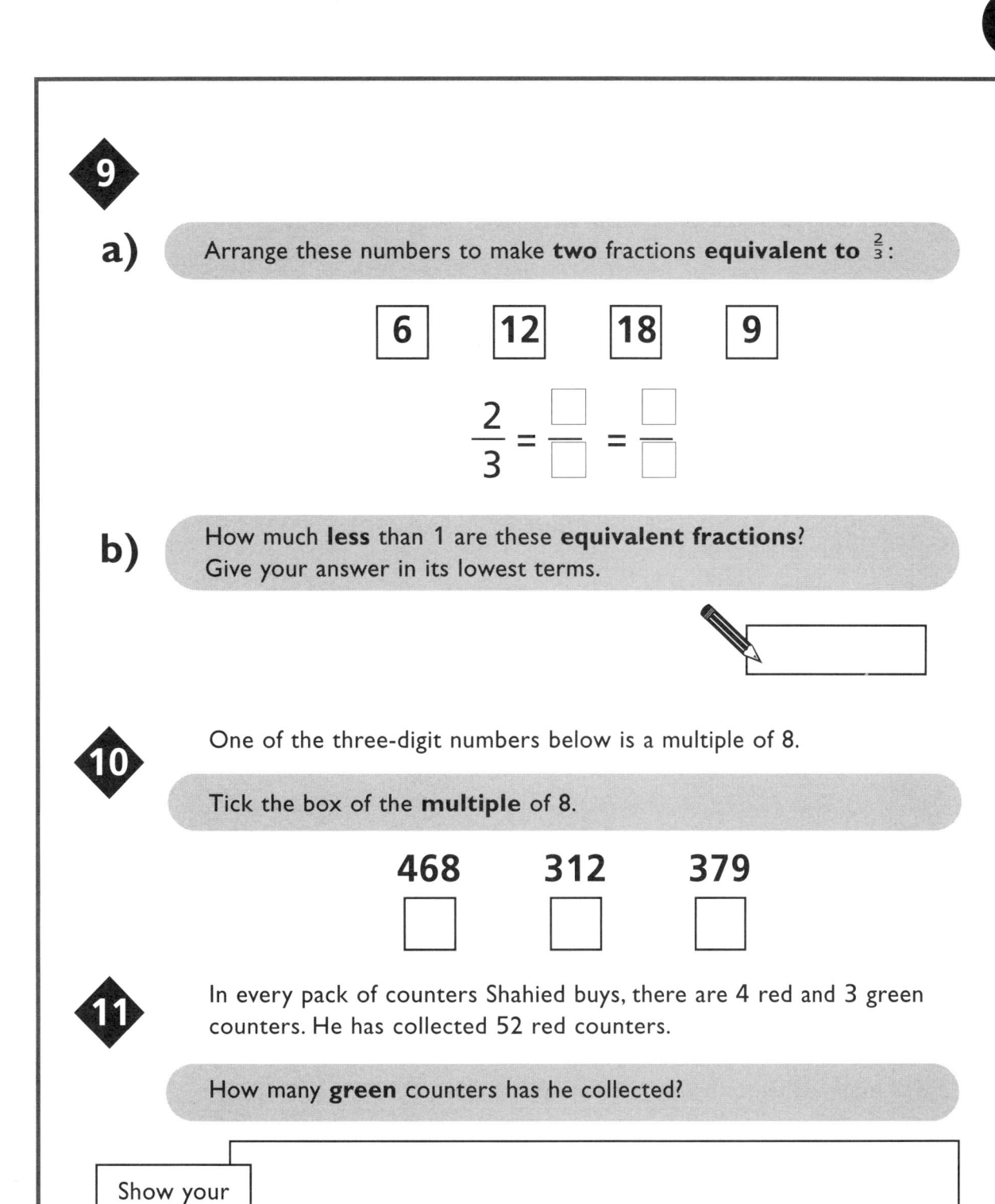

a) Arrange these numbers to make **two** fractions **equivalent to** $\frac{2}{3}$:

6   12   18   9

$$\frac{2}{3} = \frac{\square}{\square} = \frac{\square}{\square}$$

b) How much **less** than 1 are these **equivalent fractions**? Give your answer in its lowest terms.

10 One of the three-digit numbers below is a multiple of 8.

Tick the box of the **multiple** of 8.

468   312   379
☐   ☐   ☐

11 In every pack of counters Shahied buys, there are 4 red and 3 green counters. He has collected 52 red counters.

How many **green** counters has he collected?

Show your working. You may get a mark.

19

Test B

12) On the grid below, draw a shape which has 4 straight sides which are all of equal length and each longer than 4 cms. The shape must have no right angles, but the opposite sides must be parallel.

13) In this number sequence below, the numbers double.

a) Write in the missing number.

| 8 | 16 | 32 | 64 | |

In this number sequence below, the numbers treble.

b) Write in the missing number.

| | 54 | 162 | 486 | 1458 |

Here are two shapes made with centimetre squares:

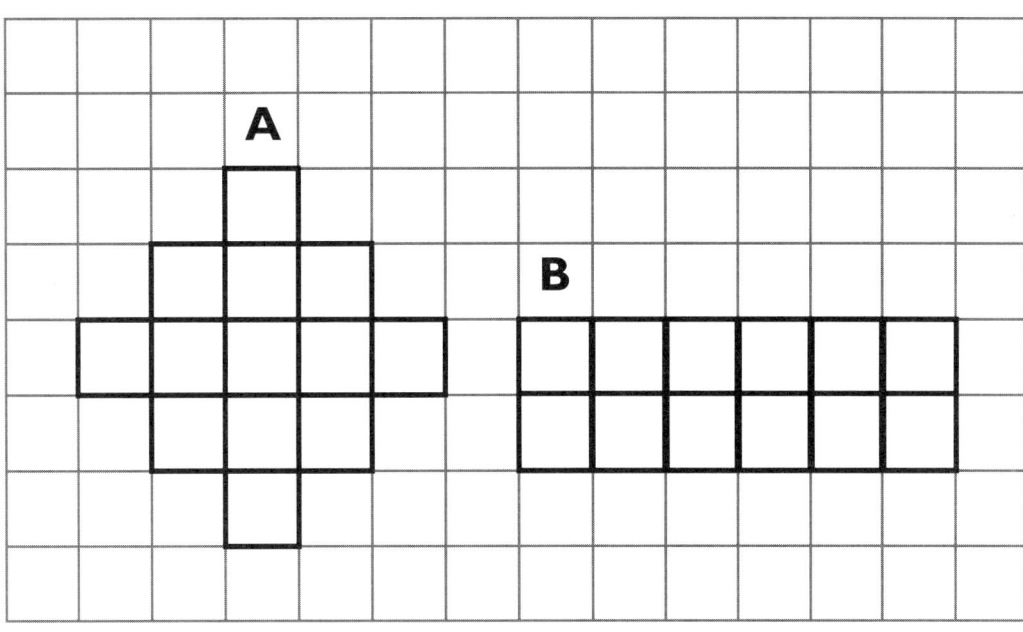

Shape A has a larger area than Shape B.

a) Explain how you can work out that Shape A has a larger area than Shape B.

_____

_____

The **perimeter** of Shape B above, is 16 cms.

b) On the grid below, draw a rectangle with a **perimeter** of 12 cms.

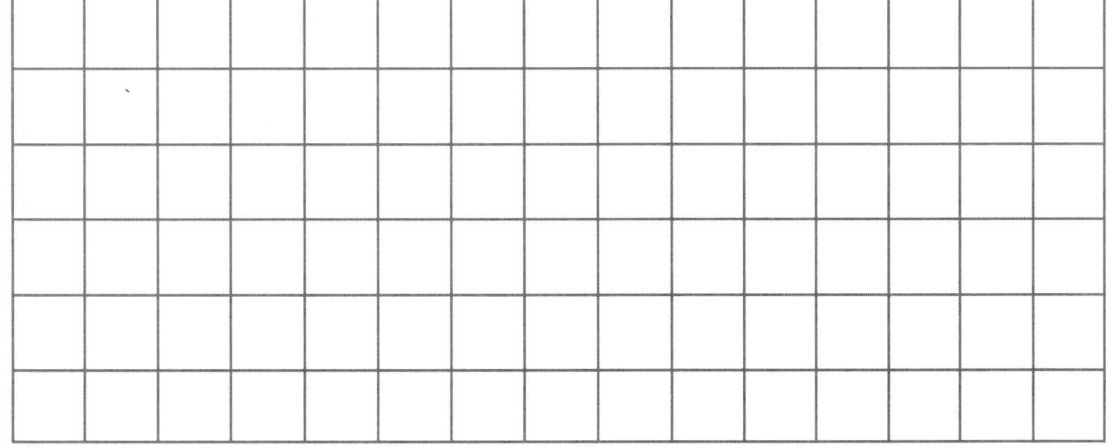

21

Test B

15 A bank provides its customers with a guide for converting pounds (£) into francs (fr.) and francs (fr.) to pounds (£).

francs (fr.)		10 fr		20 fr		30 fr	
pounds (£)	50p	£1.50	£2.50	£3.50	£4.50
	£1	£2	£3	£4

a) About how many francs are equivalent to £3.50? Give your answer to the nearest franc.

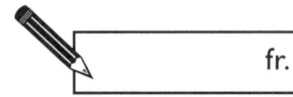
fr.

b) About how many pounds and pence are equivalent to 15 francs? Give your answer to the nearest 10 pence.

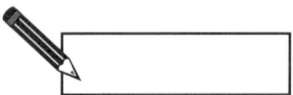

16 Mr Brown, the local shopkeeper, buys and sells jars full of mini-chocolate bars.
An empty jar costs him 35 pence and each mini-chocolate bar costs him 4 pence.
A jar full of mini-chocolate bars costs him £1.39.

a) How many mini-chocolate bars are in the jar?

Show your working. You may get a mark.

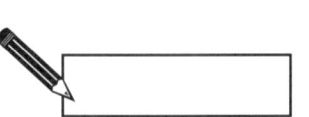

He sells each jar full of mini-chocolate bars for £1.75 and therefore makes a profit of 36p on each.

b) If he buys and sells 24 full jars, how much profit does he make altogether?

22

Here is a graph of attendance at the village football matches:

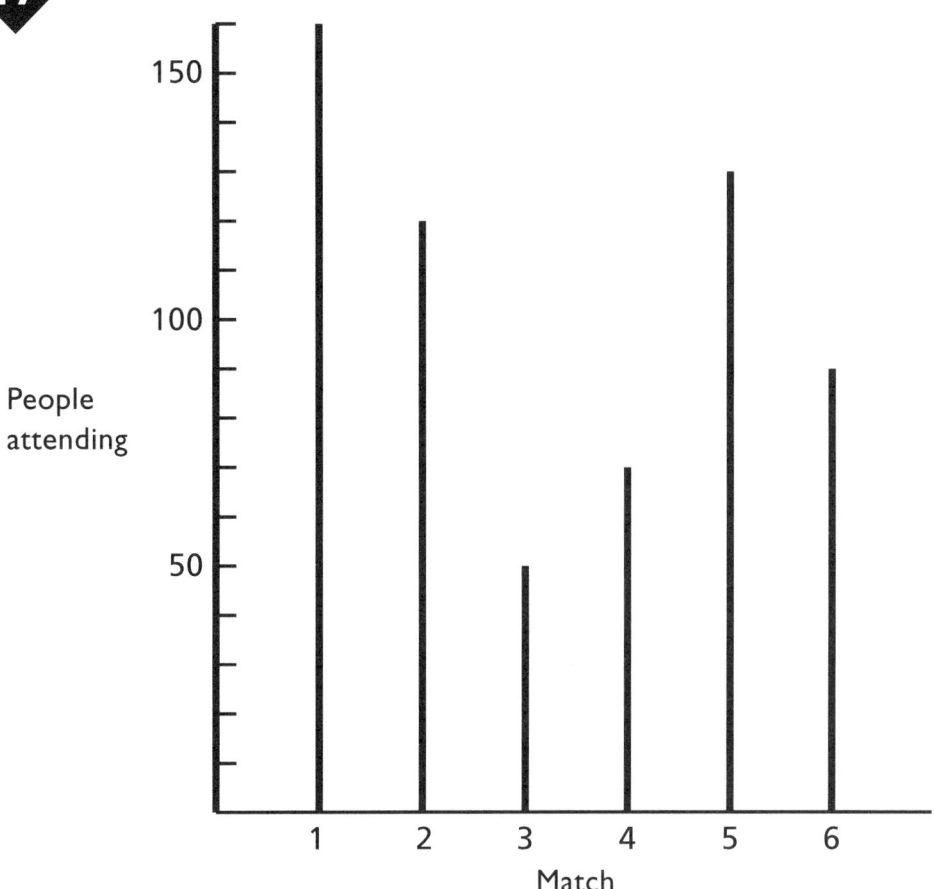

The chart below shows the changes in attendance from match to match.

Match 1 to 2	Match 2 to 3	Match 3 to 4	Match 4 to 5	Match 5 to 6
Down 40	Down 70	Up 20		

Use the graph to complete the chart.

Which match had the greatest change in attendance compared with the match before?

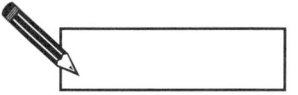

Test B

18 In a series of 6 maths tests, Jim gained:

7, 8, 3, 5, 6, 10

What is his mean - average - test mark?

19 On a plan of the school, the distance from the hall to the staff room, measures 8.4 cms.

If the scale of the plan is 1 centimetre to 8 metres, what is the walking distance - in metres - from the hall to the staff room?

m

20 Groups of children have to be accompanied by a teacher to visit the museum. The entry fees are:

Teachers 80p

Pupils 40p

a) How much will it cost 12 pupils and one teacher to visit the museum? Give your answer in pence.

Show your working. You may get a mark.

pence

b) Write a formula for the total cost of a number of pupils and a teacher to visit the museum.
c stands for the total cost of a visit of a teacher and his pupils to the museum. Let *n* be the number of pupils.

24

21 A chef keeps a record of the temperature of his two ovens during a three-hour period. He then draws a graph of the results.

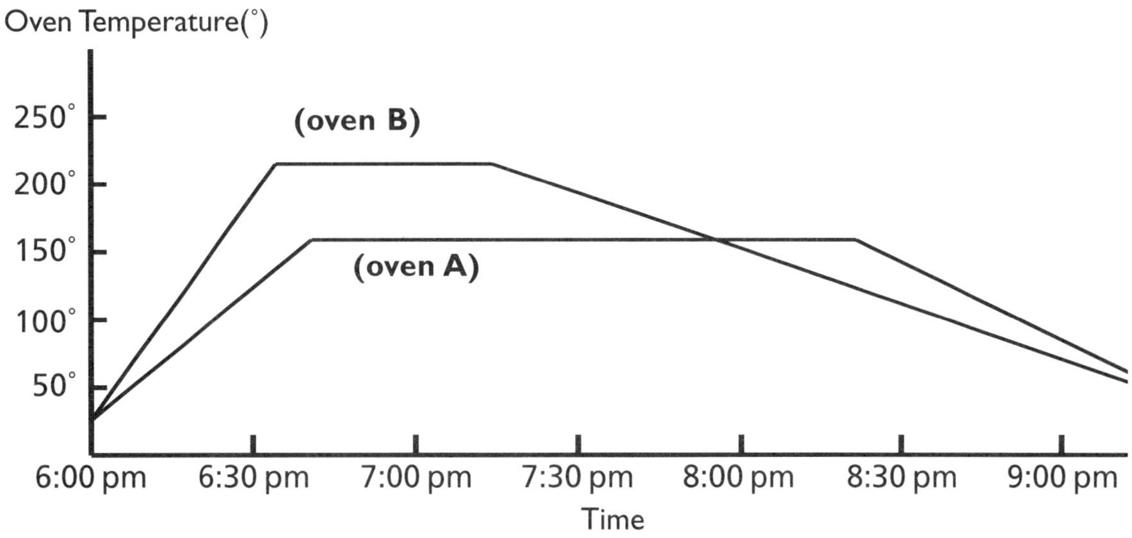

a) Estimate how much hotter oven B gets, than oven A.

1

b) Having been turned on, estimate the time when the two ovens are at the same temperature.

1

c) The chef reckons that oven A was above 100° for about $2\frac{1}{2}$ hours. Explain how the graph shows this.

1

total

Answers Test A — page 4, questions 1, 2, 3

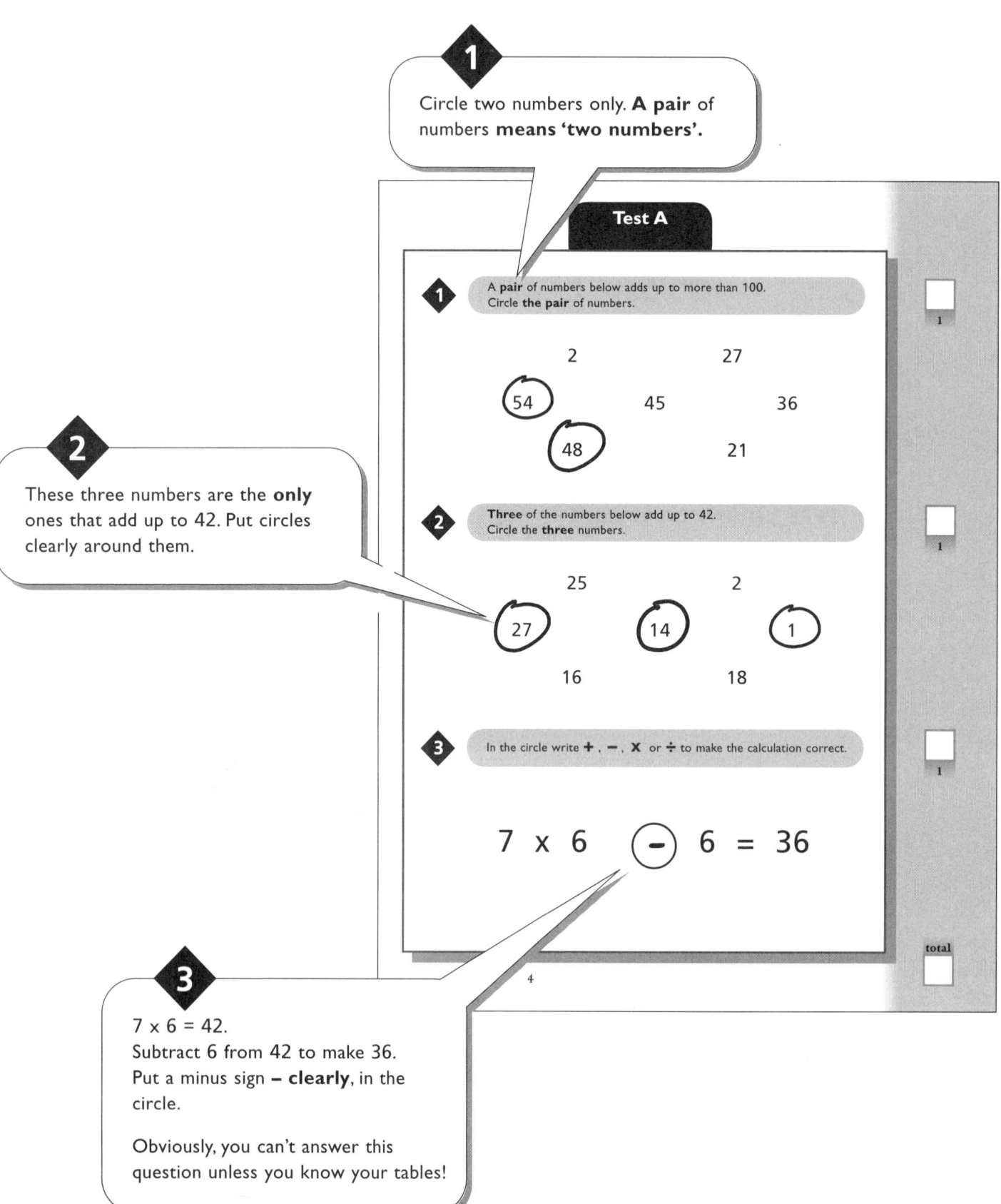

1 Circle two numbers only. **A pair** of numbers **means 'two numbers'**.

2 These three numbers are the **only** ones that add up to 42. Put circles clearly around them.

3 7 × 6 = 42.
Subtract 6 from 42 to make 36.
Put a minus sign **– clearly**, in the circle.

Obviously, you can't answer this question unless you know your tables!

26

page 5, question 4   Test A   Answers

4

a) First, read the introductory section **carefully.** Note the cost of the four special offers. Then **underline** the important points before answering the question.

Mrs Butler started with £2 and finished with 20p - so she must have spent £1.80 - the cost of one large apple pie.

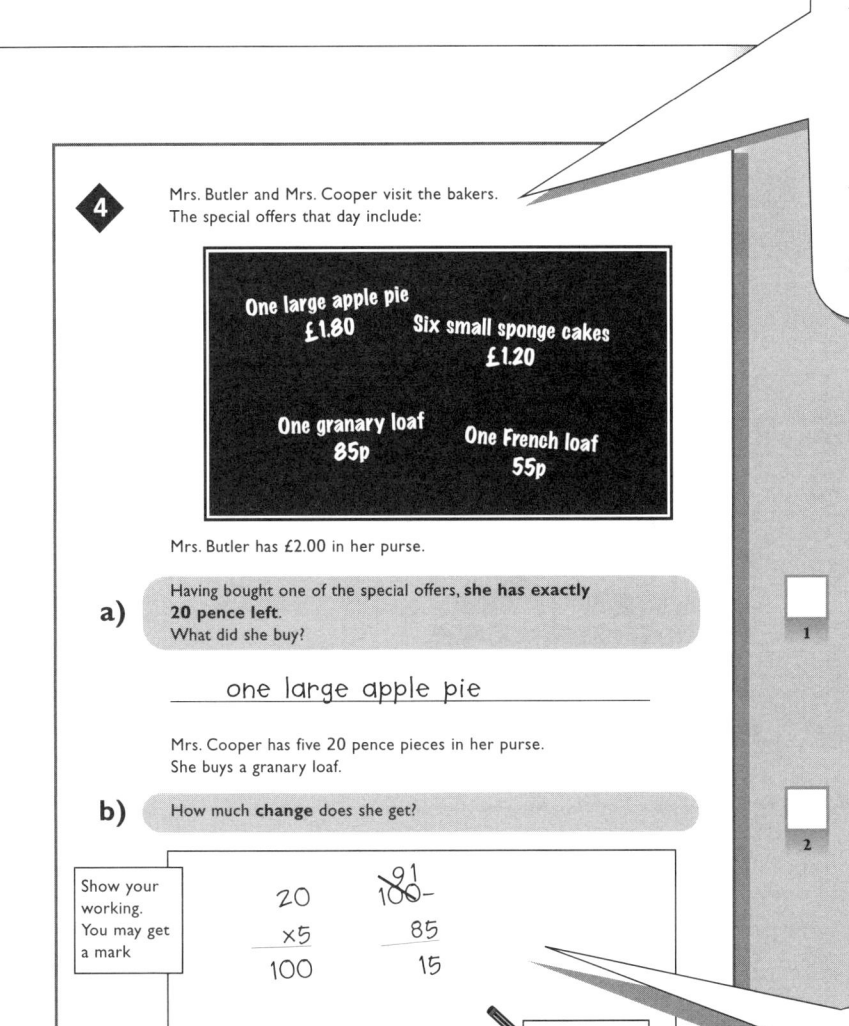

4

b) The five 20 pence pieces that Mrs Cooper has, make up £1. She spends 85 pence on the granary loaf. To find out how much change she gets, you take 85p from 100p. In the box which says: 'Show your working', you might have put:

```
        91
 20    100-
 ×5     85
100     15
```

Answers — Test A — page 6, questions 5, 6

5 a) To work out how much more Dave gets than Antonio, you have to take 40p away from £1.20.

```
  1 20p
 - 40p
 -----
   80p
```

5 b) Draw Mary's bar on the graph so that it reaches as far as 75p, that is, **half way between 70 and 80p**. The amounts listed in the table at the top, are shown in the length of the bars on the graph. For example, **Antonio,** who received the least pocket money, **has the shortest bar on the graph**. His amount reaches as far as **40p**.

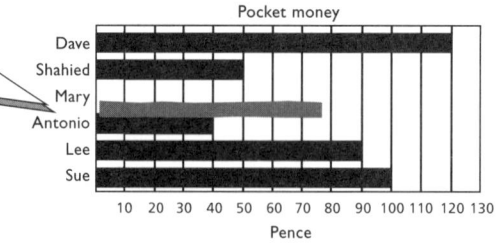

6 Your isosceles triangle should look like the one drawn here. An isosceles triangle has two of its sides equal. One of them was already drawn for you **1**. You have to draw the other equal side **2** and then the third **3**, to complete the triangle.

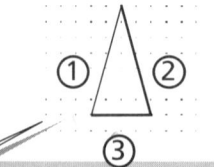

Revision Tip
The example in the question is an isosceles triangle...but, do you know what these are:

an equilateral triangle
a scalene triangle
a quadrilateral
a hexagon
a pentagon
an octagon?

And these...

a square
a rhombus
a rectangle
a parallelogram
a trapezium?

page 7, questions 7, 8 — Test A Answers

7

You need an answer in the 6 times table that ends in 8. There are two possibilities:
6 x 3 = 18
6 x 8 = 48.
If you choose 3 to go in the empty square, you will only carry 1 to the tens column. That is not enough, because 6 x 7 (42) + 1 is 43, and you need 46!
Got it wrong? Revise your tables.

7 Write in the **missing** digit.

```
  7 [8]
  x 6
  ─────
  4 6 8
```

8 A new type of trainers comes with either Ordinary Grip soles or with Special Grip soles.

They are priced as follows:

	Ordinary Grip	Special Grip
Size 1	£17.50	£18.50
Size 2	£18.25	£19.75
Size 3	£19.00	£21.00
Size 4	£19.75	£22.25
Size 5	£20.50	£23.50
Size 6	£21.25	£24.75

An extra pair of laces costs £0.75.

John buys a pair of Size 5 Special Grip Trainers and an extra pair of laces.

a) How much does John spend? £24.25

```
23.50
+ 0.75
─────
24.25
```

Gemma spends exactly £22.00 and includes a pair of laces in her purchase.

b) What trainers does she buy? size 6, ordinary grip

8

a) Pick out information from the chart that is important for answering the question:
◆ The **bigger sizes** of trainers **are more expensive.**
◆ **Special Grip Trainers are also more expensive** and, **an extra pair of laces costs 75p.**
To work out how much John spends, find the cost on the chart of:
◆ his **size - 5,**
◆ **Special Grip Trainers** and,
◆ one **extra** pair of **laces.**
For this question, you can put your working down anywhere there is space:

```
23.50
+ 0.75
─────
24.25
```

b) If Gemma **spends £22.00 altogether** and the pair of **laces costs £0.75**, she spends **£21.25** on the trainers. Check on the chart which trainers cost £21.25. Remember to use the box provided in which to write your answer. 1 mark for size 6, 1 mark for Ordinary Grip

Answers   Test A   page 8, question 9

9

a) Check whether the dotted line is a line of symmetry or not, by imagining that you are folding the shape along the dotted line. If one half **fits exactly** on the opposite half, it is a line of symmetry.
Look at figure C again. Can you see that the dotted line is not a line of symmetry? When folded along the dotted line, one half does not fit on the other half.

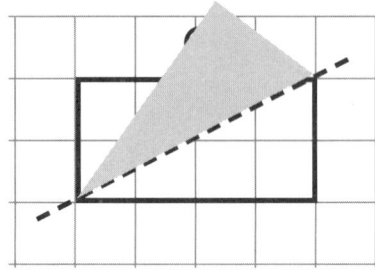

Did you know?

There is actually another way to check a line for symmetry. You can hold a mirror vertically along the dotted lines. If what you see in the mirror is not the same as that part of the drawn shape now hidden by the mirror, then the dotted line is not a line of symmetry.
Try this method with 'C'. What did you find? You should have noticed that the line seen in your mirror, is not the same as that part of the drawn shape now hidden by the mirror.

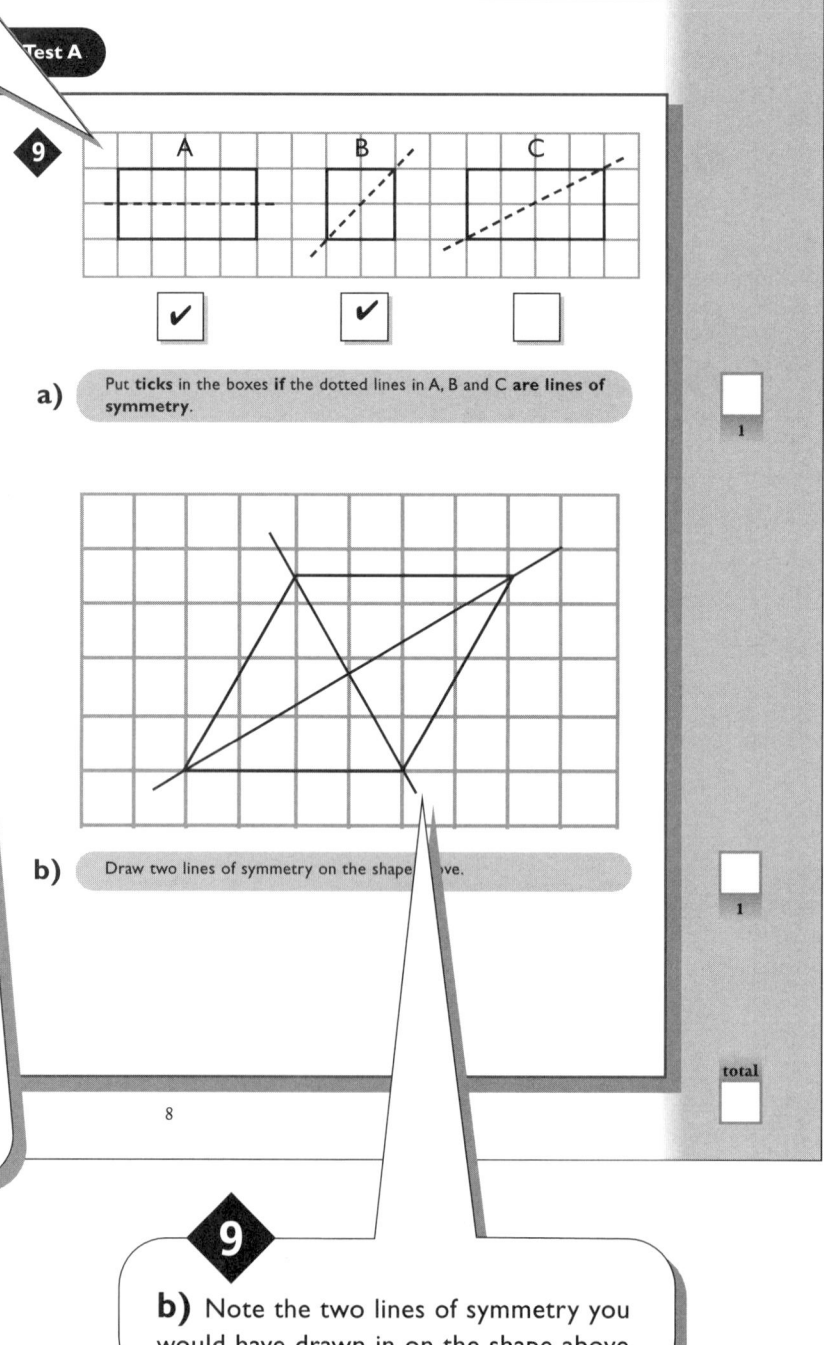

b) Note the two lines of symmetry you would have drawn in on the shape above.

30

page 9, questions 10, 11, 12 Test A Answers

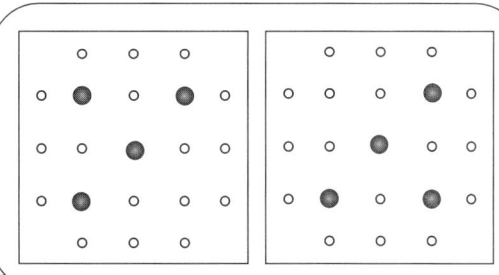

10
You will see how the marbles are repositioned, by **tracing the original position** of the marbles, and **then moving the piece of tracing paper through one right angle.**
Either of the two answers shown alongside, are correct. The trick here is to turn the page clockwise or anti-clockwise.

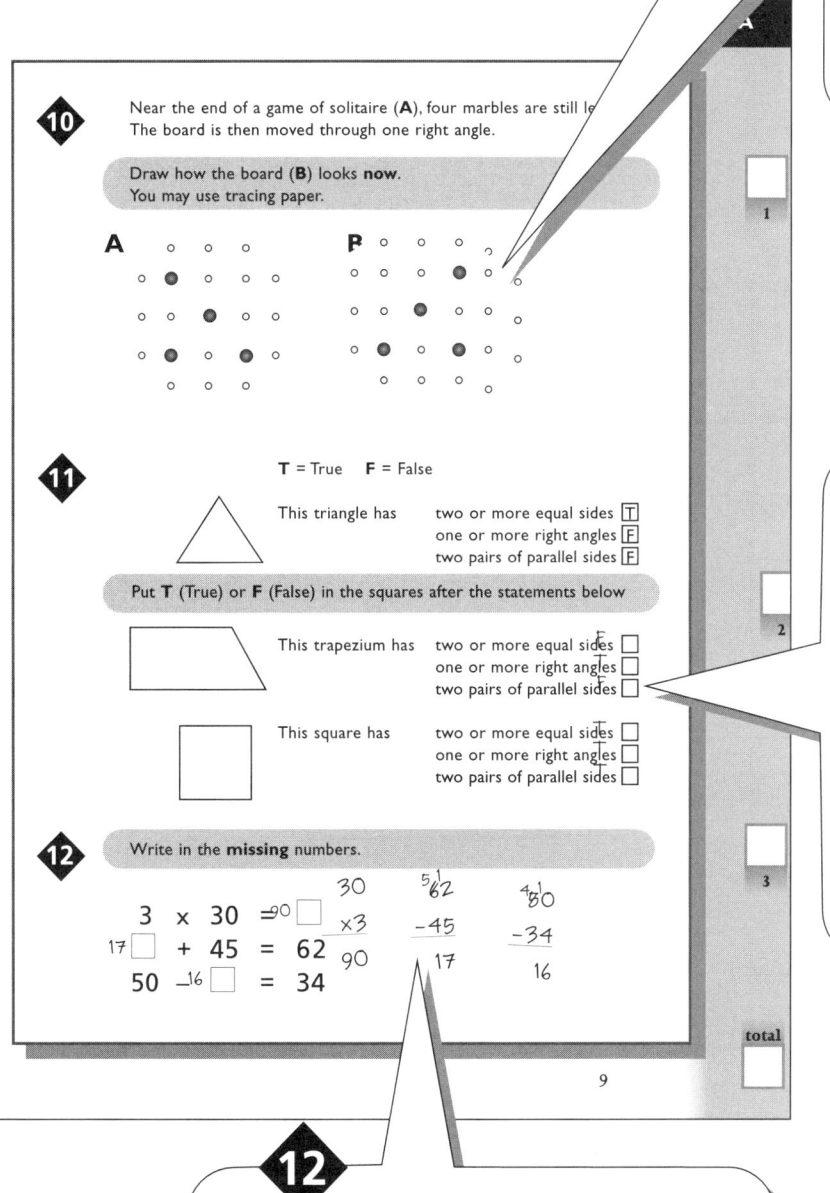

11
The trapezium has:
two or more equal sides: **F**
one or more right angles: **T**
two pairs of parallel sides: **F**

(All three must be correct for 1 mark.)

The square has:
two or more equal sides: **T**
one or more right angles: **T**
two pairs of parallel sides: **T**

(All three must be correct for 1 mark.)

12
This is quite a straightforward question. You need to demonstrate your understanding of multiplication, addition and subtraction.

31

Answers — Test A — page 10, question 13

13

a) You must **first decide** whose throw was the **longest** and whose the shortest. Then take the **smaller** measurement (14.20m - Nishma) away from the **larger** measurement (26.50m - Sara).

Remember, you were asked to give the answer in centimetres, **not** in metres!

Test A

Six children held a 'throw the tennis ball' competition. The teacher measured the distances thrown:

Name	Distance
Tom	22.75m
Jane	17.60m
Sara	26.50m
Tim	18.15m
Nishma	14.20m
Bob	15.00m

a) How much further in centimetres was the longest throw than the shortest?

Show your working. You may get a mark

```
  26.50m
 -14.20m
  12.30m
```

1230 cms

2

The children then raced back to the classroom. The teacher timed them as follows:

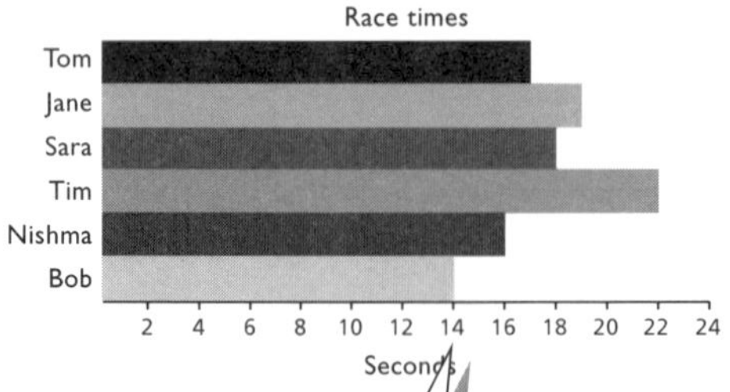

Race times

Tom, Jane, Sara, Tim, Nishma, Bob

Seconds

b) Who was the first one in the race back to the classroom?

Bob

1

total

10

13

b) Don't forget that **the fastest runner is the one** shown on the graph **to take the least amount of time.** In this case, it's Bob (14 seconds).

page 11, question 14 — Test A Answers

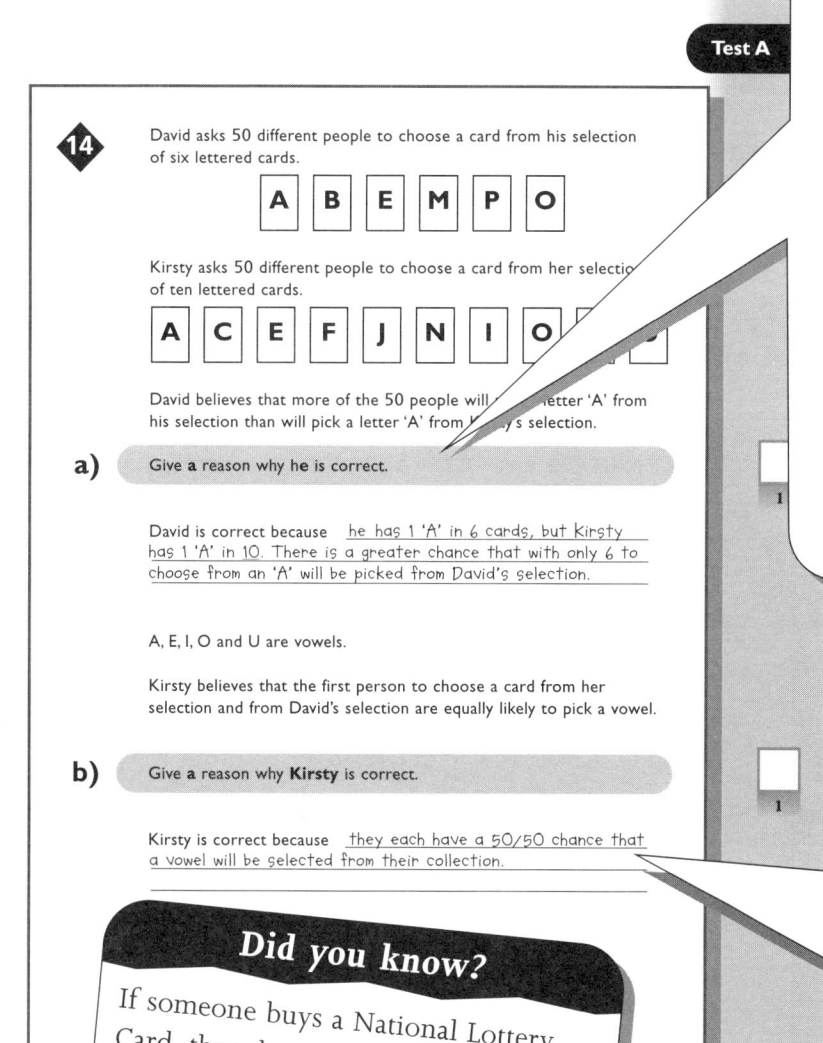

14

a) You must point out that David has one 'A' in his selection of 6 cards, whilst Kirsty has one 'A' in her selection of 10. State the probability:
  1 in 6
  1 in 10,
Then give the explanation. In 50 choices from each selection, the letter 'A' will be picked **more** times from David's than from Kirsty's selection.

Answers like these:
◆ 'It's all down to choice,' or:
◆ 'There are lots of vowels among the letters,'
are **wrong**! They don't state **probability**, they don't explain **likely outcome.**

14

b) The probability here is:
  5 out of 10 (Kirsty)
  3 out of 6 (David).
Express this mathematically as:
  ½ of Kirsty's cards
  ½ of David's cards or,
  1 out of 2.
There is an **equal** chance of a vowel being picked from either Kirsty's or David's cards.

You must refer to the fact that there is the same fraction (½), or proportion (1 in 2), or percentage (50%), of vowels in each selection, e.g. vowels make up half the letters in both. It is a 50/50 chance.

33

Answers Test A page 12, question 15

a) First, pick out the vital information.
◆ The bigger the plot, the more brussels sprouts plants grown.
◆ The number of plants per plot is twice the area, add 2
You are asked the area of a 44-plant plot. Look at the chart. It shows a pattern:
◆ Area goes up in threes.
◆ Plants go up in sixes.
You now have the information needed to answer the question. Use either of the following two methods:
1) Keep going up in threes on the chart's top line and in sixes on the chart's bottom line.

12	15	18	**21**
26	32	38	**44**

44 plants need an area of 21m²
2) Work backwards through the rule. Reverse the instructions:
44 - 2 = 42
42 ÷ 2 = 21m²

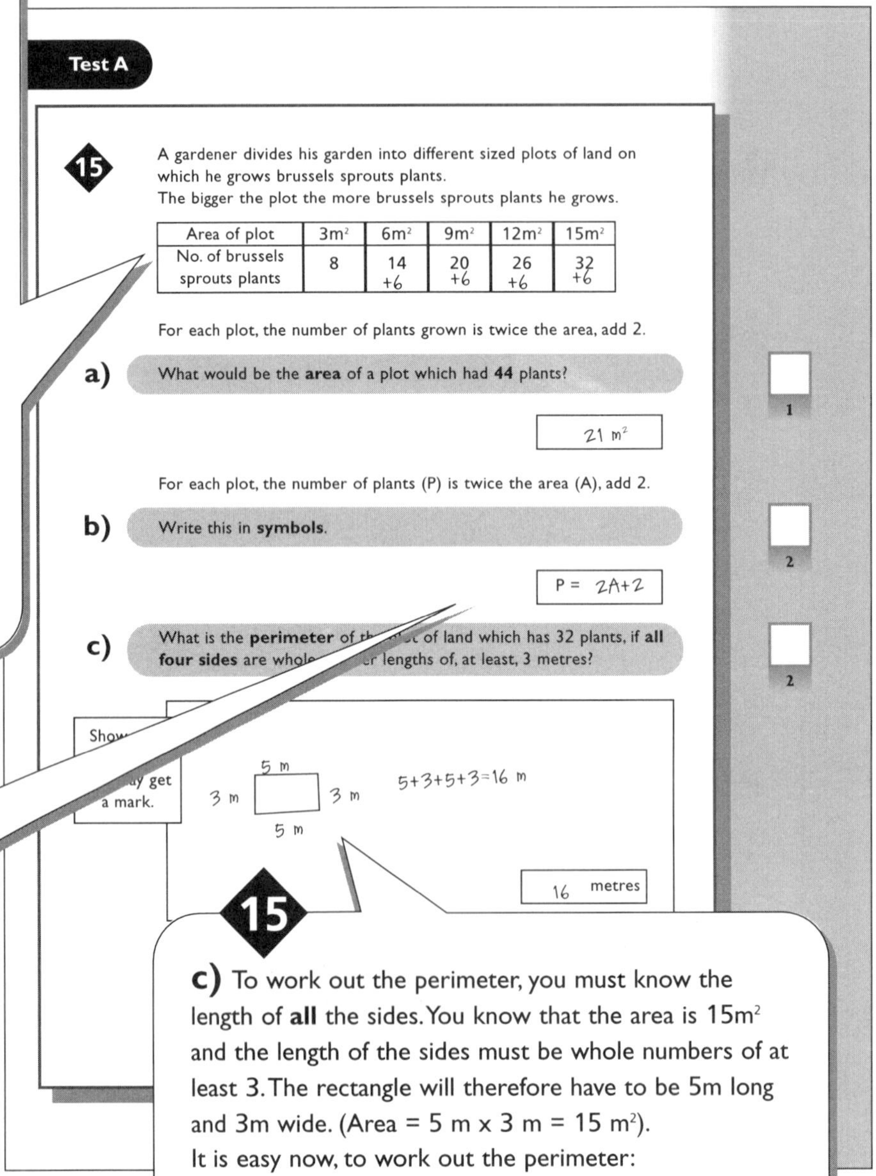

Test A

A gardener divides his garden into different sized plots of land on which he grows brussels sprouts plants.
The bigger the plot the more brussels sprouts plants he grows.

Area of plot	3m²	6m²	9m²	12m²	15m²
No. of brussels sprouts plants	8	14 +6	20 +6	26 +6	32 +6

For each plot, the number of plants grown is twice the area, add 2.

a) What would be the **area** of a plot which had **44** plants?

21 m²   [1]

For each plot, the number of plants (P) is twice the area (A), add 2.

b) Write this in **symbols**.

P = 2A+2   [2]

c) What is the **perimeter** of the plot of land which has 32 plants, if **all four sides** are whole number lengths of, at least, 3 metres?

Show ... y get a mark.

  5 m
3 m [ ] 3 m   5+3+5+3=16 m
  5 m

16 metres   [2]

b) Possible, correct answers :

P = 2A +2
or:
P = 2 × A + 2
or:
P = A + A + 2
or:
P = 2(A +1).

Two marks are given **for any one** of the answers above.
If your answer is wrong but there is evidence of 'twice the area' within the answer, e.g. 2 × A or 2A or A + A, **one mark is awarded**

c) To work out the perimeter, you must know the length of **all** the sides. You know that the area is 15m² and the length of the sides must be whole numbers of at least 3. The rectangle will therefore have to be 5m long and 3m wide. (Area = 5 m x 3 m = 15 m²).
It is easy now, to work out the perimeter:
5 + 3 + 5 + 3 = 16 metres
Well done! Take 2 marks if your answer is right. **If your answer is wrong,** you don't have to return to Go! You **still get a mark for showing that the perimeter is the sum of the four sides.**

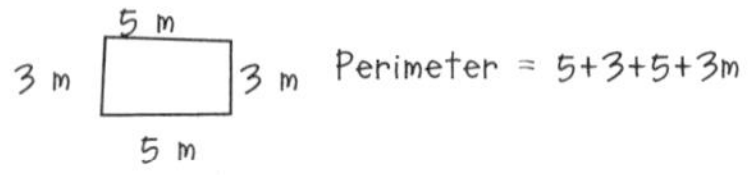

  5 m
3 m [ ] 3 m Perimeter = 5+3+5+3m
  5 m

34

page 13, questions 16, 17 — Test A — Answers

16

In any division sum, the first number is the second number multiplied by the third.
e.g. 12 ÷ 3 = 4
    12 = 3 × 4
and ☐16 ÷ 18 = 12.
    ☐16 = 12 × 18.

Therefore simply multiply 18 × 12.
```
   18
  ×12
   36
  180
  216
```
2 goes in the box.

You might like a few more examples of the rule which is described above:
♦ 28 ÷ 7 = 4.
   28 = 7 × 4 *and*,
♦ 108 ÷ 12 = 9.
   108 = 12 × 9.

16
Write in the **missing** digit.

 16 ÷ 18 = 12

17
A village is trying to raise money for new equipment on the playground. A notice is put up on the village board to show how much progress has been made.

Money still to be raised
Money promised – but not yet received
Money already received from the Council
Money already received from the villagers

a) Do you **estimate** from the diagram, that more than 50% of the money needed has already been received?
Answer yes, **or** no.

yes

b) If £1800 is needed in total, **estimate** how much money still needs to be raised. **Use the diagram to help you.**

£840.00

c) … £600 already received from the villagers, 25% came from … ow …

£150.00

total

13

17
a) You need to realise that 50% = $\frac{1}{2}$.
On the notice:
♦ 8 squares out of 15 represent money already received.
♦ 8 out of 15 is more than half (50%).
More than 50% of the money has therefore been raised.

17
b) You only have to **estimate** how much money still has to raised. Do this by looking at the notice. **Don't try to do any <u>detailed</u> calculations.**
The money that still has to be raised, is represented by 7 squares out of 15. This is less than $\frac{1}{2}$. The answer must be less than half the total money needed. Any answer of £900.00 or more, is wrong. **The precisely correct answer is £840.00**, but you only had to estimate the answer. If you estimated between £600.00 and £899.00 you earn one mark.

17
c) Dividing £600 by 4 gives you the answer: **£150.00**.
Remember:
♦ 25% means $\frac{1}{4}$.
♦ to find $\frac{1}{4}$, you divide by 4.

Revision Tip

♦ If you want to find:
$\frac{1}{3}$, divide by **3**.
$\frac{1}{8}$, divide by **8**.
$\frac{1}{10}$, divide by **10**.

♦ If you want to find:
$\frac{2}{3}$, divide by **3** and then multiply by **2**.
$\frac{3}{8}$, divide by **8** and then multiply by **3**.
$\frac{7}{10}$, divide by **10** and then multiply by **7**.
Give yourself some examples to check if you have understood this:
♦ $\frac{2}{3}$ of 12 = ?
♦ $\frac{3}{8}$ of 16 = ?

Answers Test A   page 14, questions 18, 19

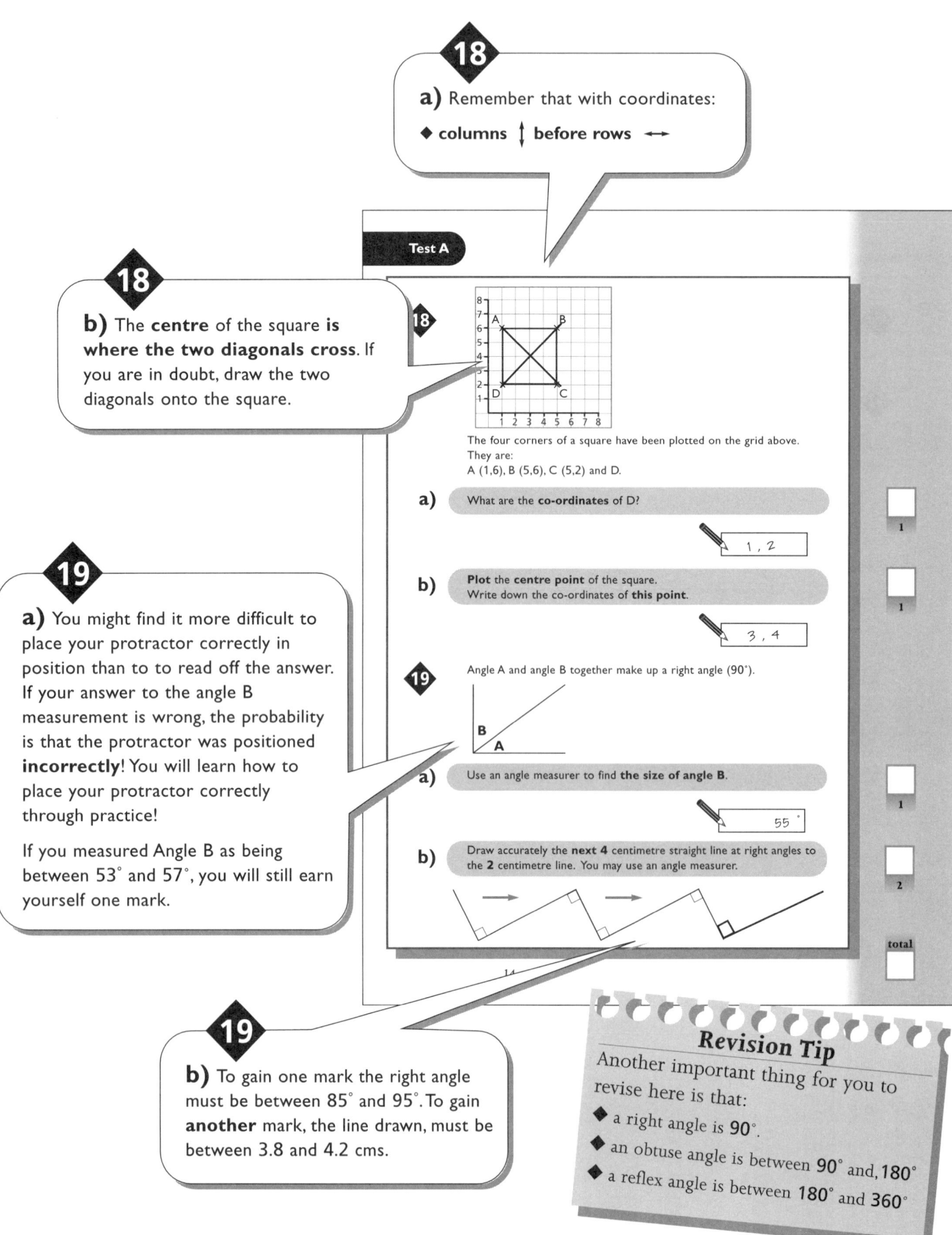

18

a) Remember that with coordinates:
- columns ↕ before rows ↔

18

b) The **centre** of the square **is where the two diagonals cross**. If you are in doubt, draw the two diagonals onto the square.

19

a) You might find it more difficult to place your protractor correctly in position than to to read off the answer. If your answer to the angle B measurement is wrong, the probability is that the protractor was positioned **incorrectly**! You will learn how to place your protractor correctly through practice!

If you measured Angle B as being between 53° and 57°, you will still earn yourself one mark.

19

b) To gain one mark the right angle must be between 85° and 95°. To gain **another** mark, the line drawn, must be between 3.8 and 4.2 cms.

Revision Tip

Another important thing for you to revise here is that:
- a right angle is **90°**.
- an obtuse angle is between **90°** and **180°**
- a reflex angle is between **180°** and **360°**

page 15, questions 1, 2 — Test B Answers

1

a) You need to know your basic numbers well to answer this question. By basic numbers we mean:
- hundreds
- tens *and*,
- units.

Test B

1 7 1 4

147 is the smallest number that can be made by arranging the three digits above.

a) What is the **largest** number that can be made by rearranging the three digits?

741

b) Using **all** the digits, write a number which is an **even** number.

174

2 John spends 87p at the shop. He gives the shopkeeper a £1 coin. He receives 3 coins as change.

What were the 3 coins?

10p   2p   1p

Did you know?

The following tips will help you to answer this **type** of question:
- **Even numbers** always divide by two with no remainder.
- **Even numbers** always end in **0, 2, 4, 6** or **8**. For example, **1,472** is an even number.
- **Odd numbers** always end in **1, 3, 5, 7** or, **9**.
- **Odd numbers** always have a remainder of one when divided by two. For example, **2,465** is an odd number.

2 John gets 13p change from his £1 coin. So, the coins in his change are: 10p; 2p; 1p.

You may, of course, use a calculator on Paper B. You should be able to calculate 100 - 87 mentally but if you wish, write the sum down or use a calculator.

37

Answers Test B page 16, question 3

3

a) You need to realise that the number of children doing an activity on a particular **day** is shown in a particular **rectangle** on the chart.
Where the computing column ↕ meets the Thursday row ↔, you will find the number (12) telling you how many did computing on that Thursday. The activity shown is:
- computing
- on Thursdays.

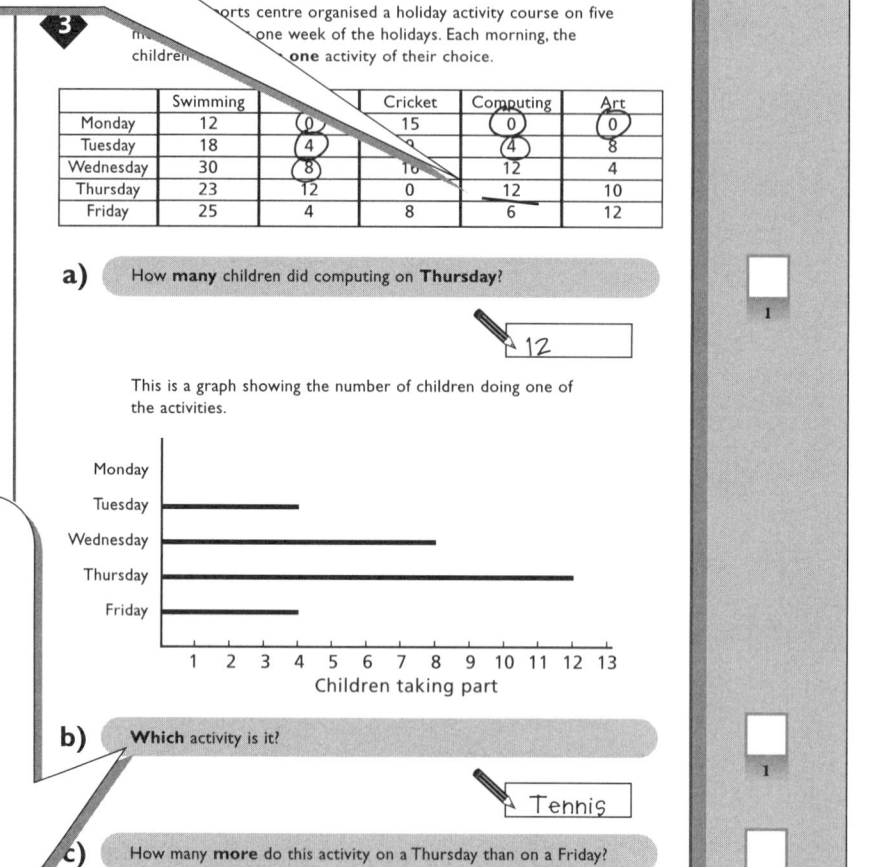

3

b) Find out which activity the graph shows by using the chart **and** the graph.

Monday:
Graph – Nobody does this activity.
Chart – The possibilities are:
- Tennis - 0
- Computing - 0
- Art - 0.

Tuesday:
Graph – Four people do this activity.
Chart – The possibilities now are:
- Tennis - 4
- Computing - 4

Art is ruled out - 8 do it on Tuesdays.

Wednesday:
Graph – Eight people do this activity.
Chart – The only activity that 8 people follow is:
- Tennis.

3

c) 12 take part in Tennis on Thursday.
4 take part in Tennis on Friday.
Therefore 8 more (12 − 4) take part in tennis on Thursday than Friday.

page 17, questions 4, 5, 6, 7 — Test B — Answers

Questions 4, 5, 6, 7 are all very similar, because they require you to be agile with basic numbers - the tens, hundreds and units.

4

Arrive at this answer by doing mental calculations, or by writing the numbers down and doing subtraction sums. **A calculator could help you.**

4 The teacher has written these numbers on the board. The pair of linked numbers has a difference of 9.

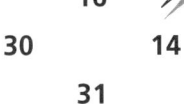

17   36   16
41   23   30   14
3   26   31

Write in the boxes below **the other pair of numbers** with a difference of 9.

5 Write in the boxes below the two numbers from those written on the board in question 4 which will divide by 4 with no remainder.

6 Write in the **missing** digits.

```
  ☐ 5 5
- 1 8 ☐
  3 7 4
```

7 A jar contains 260 sweets. They are shared equally among 10 children.

How many does **each** child get?

26 sweets

5

If you are familiar with your 4 times tables, you will have an advantage in quickly spotting the two numbers. You can take more time to answer though, by dividing each number by 4 - possibly by using your calculator.

6

The following method is used:
◆ Take 1 from 5 to get 4 in the **units** column.
◆ 8 cannot be taken from 5 in the tens column, so 1 has to be borrowed from the 5 in the **hundreds** column.
◆ Now, 1 can be subtracted from 4 to give 3.

Both squares must be completed correctly for one mark.

7

When multiplying any whole number by 10, simply add a nought (0). When dividing any whole number ending in 0 by ten, knock off the nought (0). For this answer, take 0 off 260 to give you 26.

Answers Test B — page 18, question 8

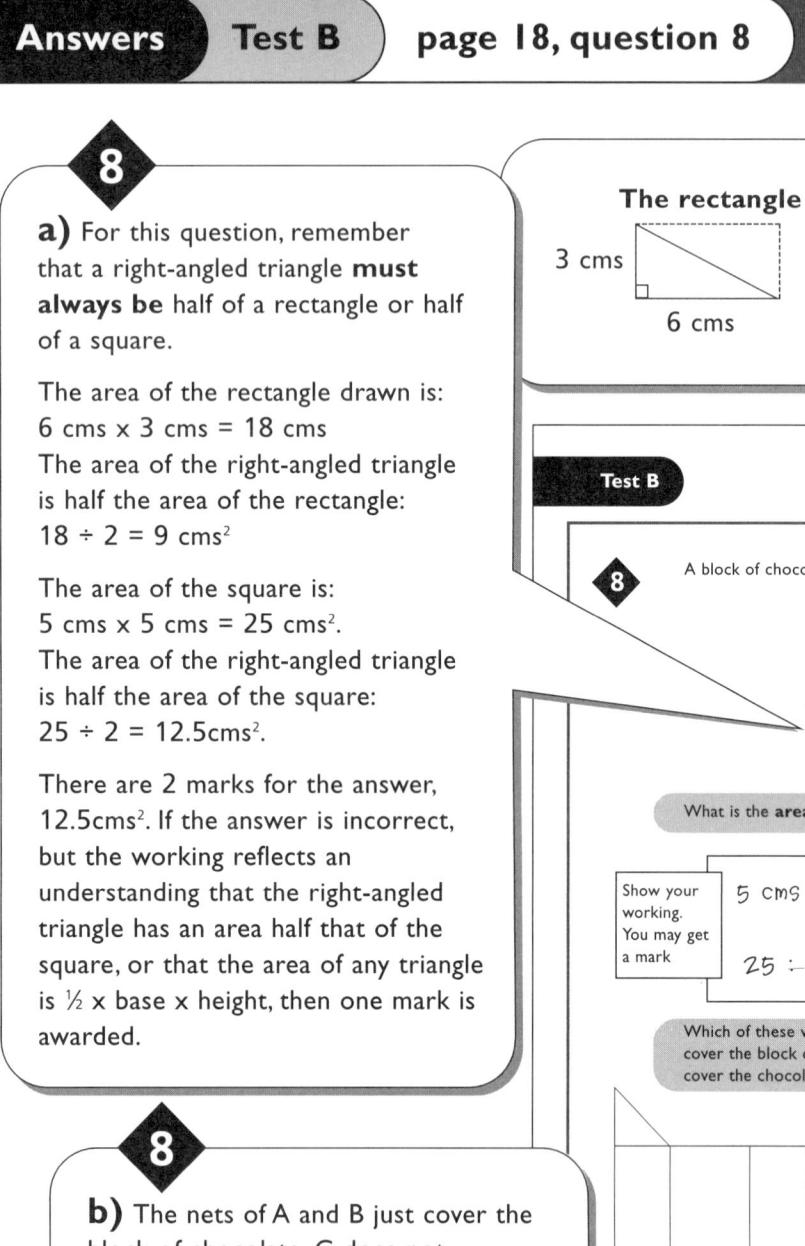

8

a) For this question, remember that a right-angled triangle **must always be** half of a rectangle or half of a square.

The area of the rectangle drawn is:
6 cms x 3 cms = 18 cms
The area of the right-angled triangle is half the area of the rectangle:
18 ÷ 2 = 9 cms^2

The area of the square is:
5 cms x 5 cms = 25 cms^2.
The area of the right-angled triangle is half the area of the square:
25 ÷ 2 = 12.5cms^2.

There are 2 marks for the answer, 12.5cms^2. If the answer is incorrect, but the working reflects an understanding that the right-angled triangle has an area half that of the square, or that the area of any triangle is ½ x base x height, then one mark is awarded.

The rectangle
3 cms
6 cms

The square
5 cms
5 cms

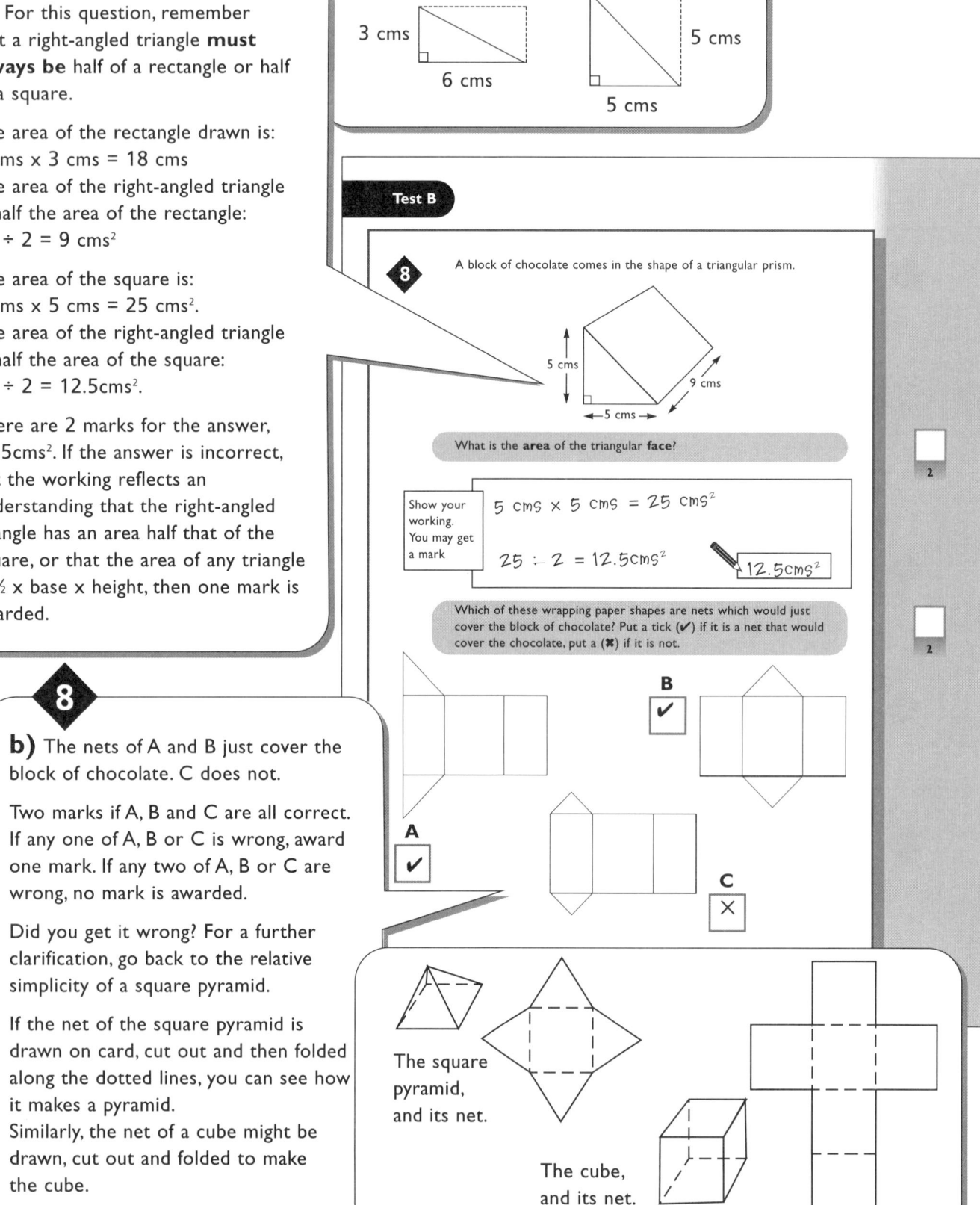

Test B

8 A block of chocolate comes in the shape of a triangular prism.

5 cms
5 cms
9 cms

What is the **area** of the triangular **face**?

Show your working. You may get a mark

5 cms x 5 cms = 25 cms^2
25 ÷ 2 = 12.5cms^2

12.5cms^2

[2]

Which of these wrapping paper shapes are nets which would just cover the block of chocolate? Put a tick (✔) if it is a net that would cover the chocolate, put a (✘) if it is not.

A ✔
B ✔
C ✘

[2]

8

b) The nets of A and B just cover the block of chocolate. C does not.

Two marks if A, B and C are all correct. If any one of A, B or C is wrong, award one mark. If any two of A, B or C are wrong, no mark is awarded.

Did you get it wrong? For a further clarification, go back to the relative simplicity of a square pyramid.

If the net of the square pyramid is drawn on card, cut out and then folded along the dotted lines, you can see how it makes a pyramid.
Similarly, the net of a cube might be drawn, cut out and folded to make the cube.

The square pyramid, and its net.

The cube, and its net.

40

page 19, questions 9, 10, 11 — **Test B** — **Answers**

9

a) To find the fraction **equivalent** to $\frac{2}{3}$, multiply the numerator and the denominator by the **same** number:

$\frac{2}{3}\stackrel{\times 2}{=}\frac{4}{6}$, $\frac{2}{3}\stackrel{\times 3}{=}\frac{6}{9}$, $\frac{2}{3}\stackrel{\times 4}{=}\frac{8}{12}$, $\frac{2}{3}\stackrel{\times 5}{=}\frac{10}{15}$, $\frac{2}{3}\stackrel{\times 6}{=}\frac{12}{18}$.

The equivalent fractions using 6, 12, 18 and 9 are therefore:
$\frac{2}{3} = \frac{6}{9} = \frac{12}{18}$.

9

a) Arrange these numbers to make **two** fractions equivalent to $\frac{2}{3}$:

$\boxed{6}\quad \boxed{12}\quad \boxed{18}\quad \boxed{9}$

$\frac{2}{3} = \frac{\boxed{6}}{\boxed{9}} = \frac{\boxed{12}}{\boxed{18}}$

b) How much **less** than 1 are these **equivalent fractions**? Give your answer in its lowest terms.

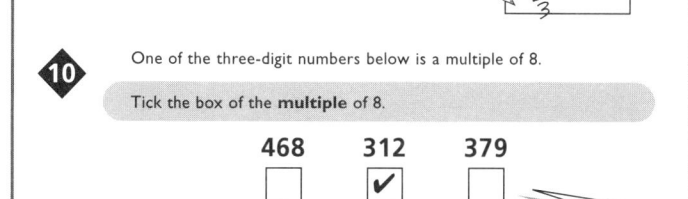

$\boxed{\frac{1}{3}}$

9

b) These equivalent fractions are $\frac{1}{3}$ less than 1, $\frac{3}{9}$ less than 1 and $\frac{6}{18}$ less than 1. In lowest terms the answer is $\frac{1}{3}$.

10

One of the three-digit numbers below is a multiple of 8.

Tick the box of the **multiple** of 8.

468 □   312 ✓   379 □

10

For a number to be a multiple of 8, you must be able to divide that number by 8 **with no remainder**.

$8\overline{)468} = 58R4$ $8\overline{)312} = 39$ $8\overline{)379} = 47R3$

11

In every pack of counters Shahied buys, there are 4 red and 3 green counters. He has collected 52 red counters.

How many **green** counters has he collected?

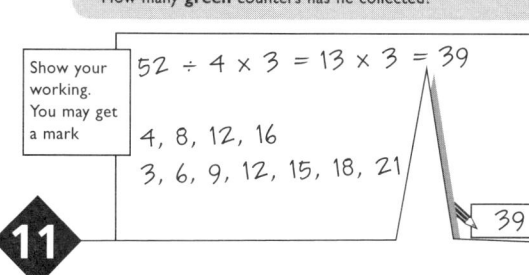

Show your working. You may get a mark:

$52 \div 4 \times 3 = 13 \times 3 = 39$

4, 8, 12, 16
3, 6, 9, 12, 15, 18, 21

$\boxed{39}$

11

If for every 4 red ones in the pack, there are 3 green ones, then the ratio is 4:3.
Find out how many green counters he has collected, by dividing 52 by 4 (=13) and then multiplying by 3 (13 × 3 = 39)

Or, **build on the principle of ratio** by going up in 4's and 3's until you reach 52 red ones.
The equivalent number of green is 39.

red :   4, 8, 12, 16 → 52
green : 3, 6, 9, 12 → 39.

41

Answers — Test B — page 20, questions 12, 13

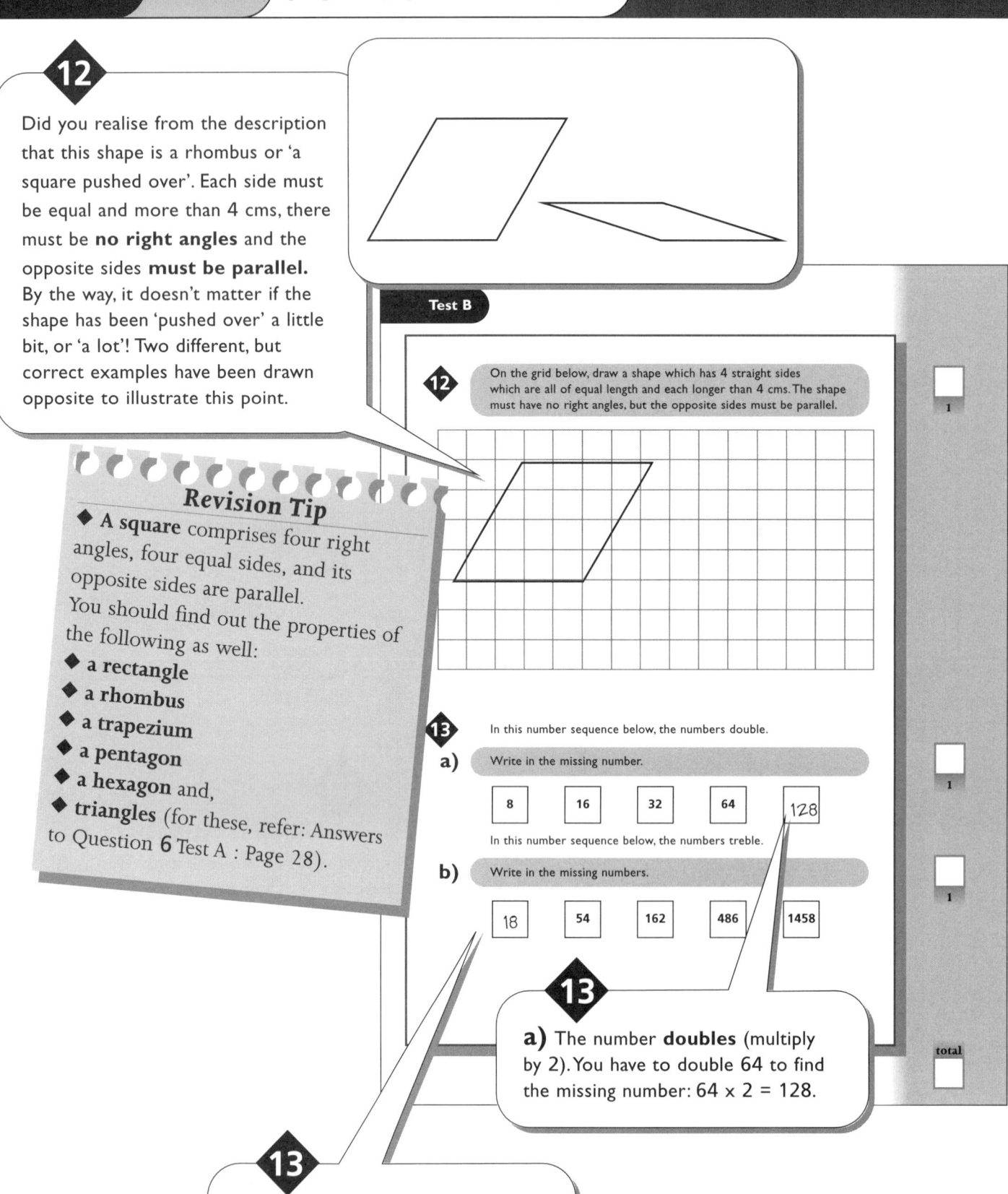

12

Did you realise from the description that this shape is a rhombus or 'a square pushed over'. Each side must be equal and more than 4 cms, there must be **no right angles** and the opposite sides **must be parallel.** By the way, it doesn't matter if the shape has been 'pushed over' a little bit, or 'a lot'! Two different, but correct examples have been drawn opposite to illustrate this point.

Revision Tip

◆ **A square** comprises four right angles, four equal sides, and its opposite sides are parallel. You should find out the properties of the following as well:

◆ a rectangle
◆ a rhombus
◆ a trapezium
◆ a pentagon
◆ a hexagon and,
◆ triangles (for these, refer: Answers to Question 6 Test A : Page 28).

Test B

12 On the grid below, draw a shape which has 4 straight sides which are all of equal length and each longer than 4 cms. The shape must have no right angles, but the opposite sides must be parallel.

13 In this number sequence below, the numbers double.

a) Write in the missing number.

| 8 | 16 | 32 | 64 | 128 |

In this number sequence below, the numbers treble.

b) Write in the missing numbers.

| 18 | 54 | 162 | 486 | 1458 |

13

a) The number **doubles** (multiply by 2). You have to double 64 to find the missing number: 64 × 2 = 128.

13

b) The number **trebles** (multiply by 3). You have to work **backwards** along the line and **divide** 54 by 3 to find the missing numbers: 54 ÷ 3 = 18.

42

page 21, question 14 — **Test B** — **Answers**

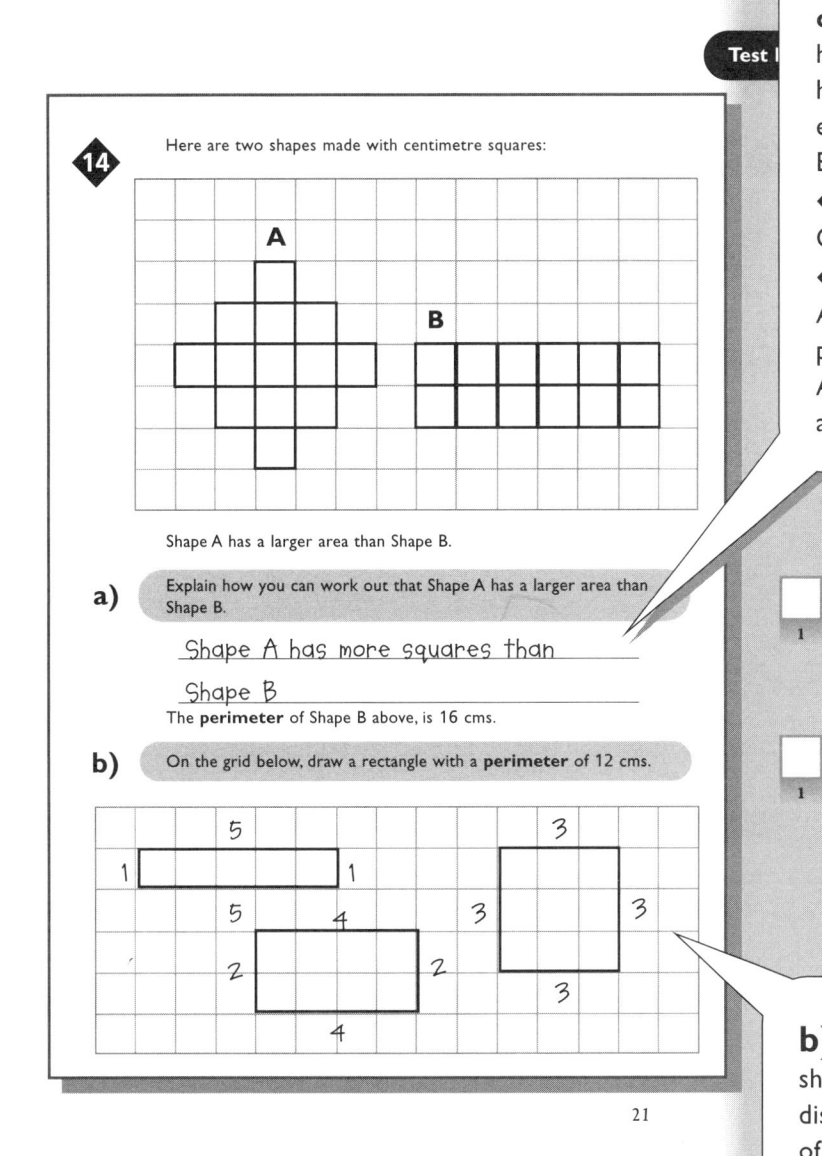

14

a) Any answer which shows that you understand the concept, or idea, of area, in other words, '**surface covered**'; and which also explains how you can work out that Shape A has a larger area than Shape B, will earn you one mark.
Examples of correct answers are:
◆ A has more squares than B.
Or,
◆ By adding up the squares..... .
Any answer which refers to perimeter, sides or edges **is wrong**. Area is surface covered, **not** distance along lines.

14

b) Three possible answers are shown here. The perimeter is the distance all the way round the outside of a shape. You need to draw a rectangle where 4 sides add up to a total length of 12 cms.

---

14 Here are two shapes made with centimetre squares:

Shape A has a larger area than Shape B.

a) Explain how you can work out that Shape A has a larger area than Shape B.

Shape A has more squares than Shape B

The **perimeter** of Shape B above, is 16 cms.

b) On the grid below, draw a rectangle with a **perimeter** of 12 cms.

21

43

Answers Test B — page 22, questions 15, 16

15

a) You must locate £3.50 on the lower section and note that the equivalent sum in francs, is between 26 and 27. It is, however, closer to 27 than 26, and the answer to 'the nearest franc' is 27. You might like to look at a conversion chart displayed at your nearest petrol station. It will show the cost of petrol in litres and gallons.

15

b) To the nearest 10 pence', means either 10p, or 20p, 30p, 40p, or £1.20, £1.30, £1.40, and so on. You will see that 15fr comes very close to £2. The answer should be given as £2.00 or £2 or 200p.

16

a) Take particular note of each sentence like this:
- 'The jar full of mini-chocolate bars costs the shopkeeper £1.39.'
- 'An empty jar costs the shopkeeper 35p'.

So to find the cost of the mini-chocolate bars, 35p is subtracted from £1.39.

```
 139
 -35
 104p
```

104p is the cost of the mini-chocolate bars at 4p each. Divide the total cost of the bars (104p) by the cost of one bar (4p) to find the number of bars in the jar.

The answer 26 gains 2 marks
If your final answer was wrong or missing but you showed correct working, e.g.
139 − 35 = 104 and 104 ÷ 4 = 26
1 mark is awarded.

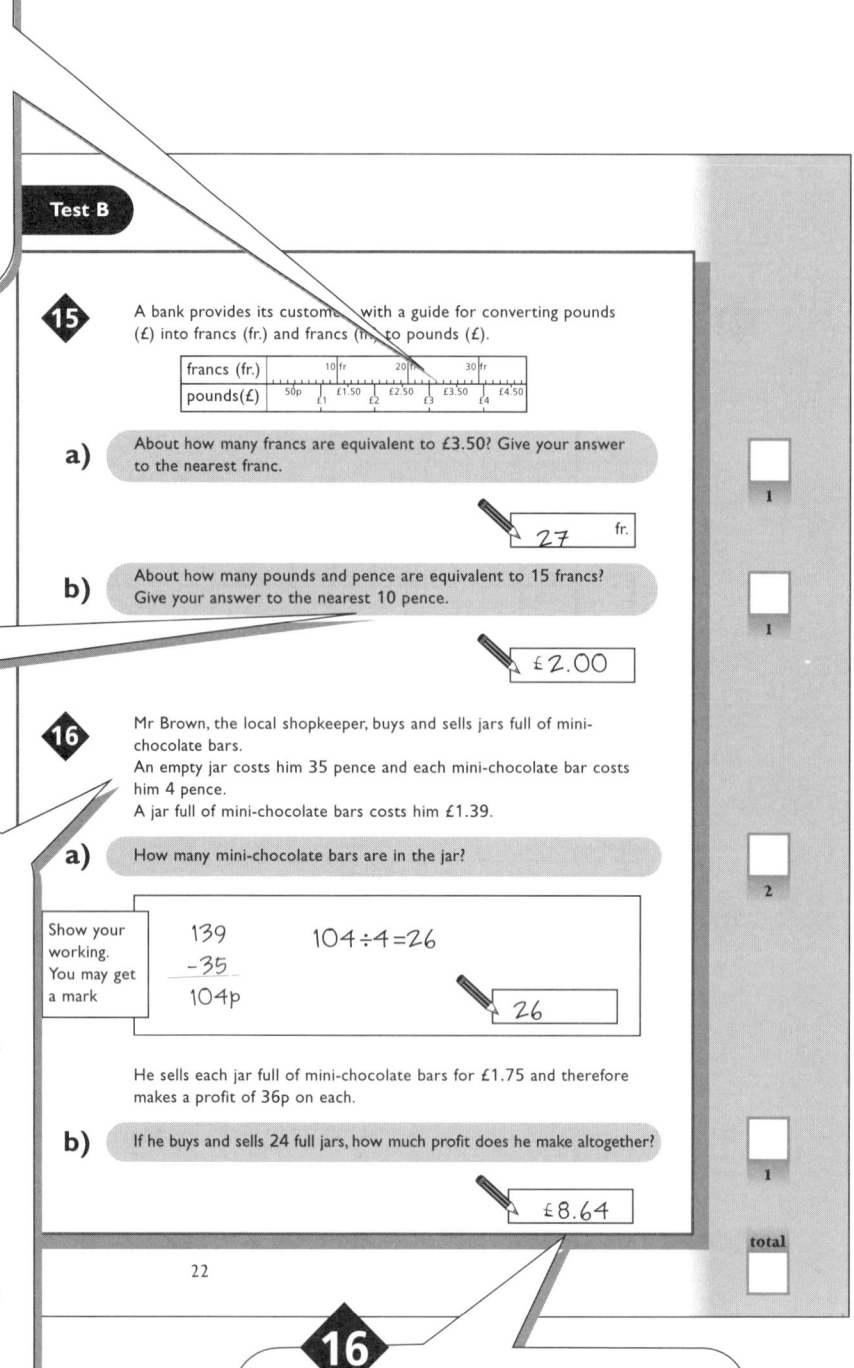

16

b) The shopkeeper makes a profit of 36p on each jar. He buys and sells 24 jars and the total profit is calculated by multiplying 36 × 24. The profit he makes altogether is £8.64 (or 864p).

Test B

15 A bank provides its customers with a guide for converting pounds (£) into francs (fr.) and francs (fr.) to pounds (£).

francs (fr.)		10 fr		20 fr		30 fr	
pounds (£)	50p	£1.50	£2	£2.50	£3	£3.50	£4.50
	£1					£4	

a) About how many francs are equivalent to £3.50? Give your answer to the nearest franc.

27 fr.

b) About how many pounds and pence are equivalent to 15 francs? Give your answer to the nearest 10 pence.

£2.00

16 Mr Brown, the local shopkeeper, buys and sells jars full of mini-chocolate bars.
An empty jar costs him 35 pence and each mini-chocolate bar costs him 4 pence.
A jar full of mini-chocolate bars costs him £1.39.

a) How many mini-chocolate bars are in the jar?

Show your working. You may get a mark

```
 139
 -35
 104p       104÷4=26
```

26

He sells each jar full of mini-chocolate bars for £1.75 and therefore makes a profit of 36p on each.

b) If he buys and sells 24 full jars, how much profit does he make altogether?

£8.64

44

page 23, question 17 — Test B Answers

17

Here is a graph of attendance at the village football matches:

[Graph showing People attending on y-axis (0 to 150+) vs Match number 1–6 on x-axis]

The chart below shows the changes in attendance from match to match.

Match 1 to 2	Match 2 to 3	Match 3 to 4	Match 4 to 5	Match 5 to 6
Down 40	Down 70	Up 20	Up 60	Down 40

Use the graph to complete the chart.

Which match had the greatest change in attendance compared with the match before?

Match 3

17

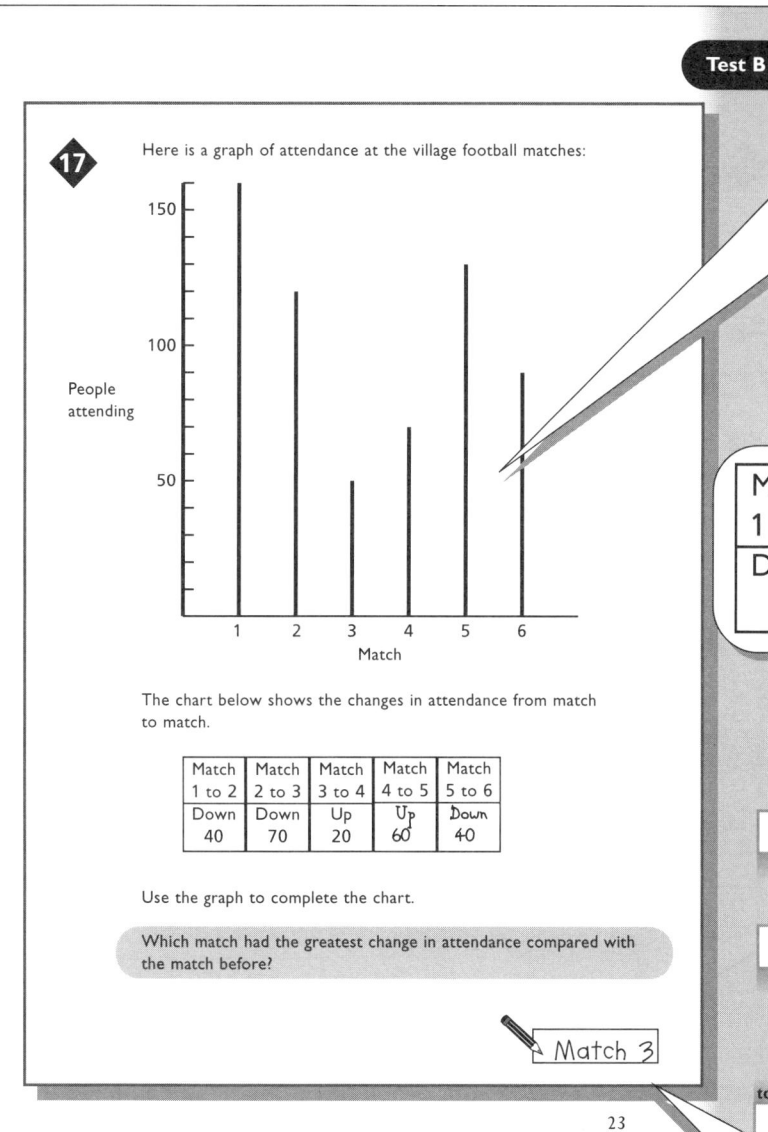

Note the attendances of matches 4, 5 and 6 **from the graph**:

- **Match 4** - 70 } up 60
- **Match 5** - 130 } down 40
- **Match 6** - 90

Your answer would have been shown like this:

Match 1 to 2	Match 2 to 3	Match 3 to 4	Match 4 to 5	Match 5 to 6
Down 40	Down 70	Up 20	Up 60	Down 40

It can be shown that the greatest change in attendance was 'down 70' (Match 2 to 3), so that the match with the greatest attendance compared with the match before was **Match 3**.

Answers — Test B — page 24, questions 18, 19, 20

18

Calculate the **average** or mean, by dividing the sum of the numbers (7+8+3+5+6+10 = 39) by how many numbers there are (6). In other words, $6\overline{)39}$. But **39 does not divide exactly by 6**, and the remainder must be dealt with to give a fraction answer or a decimal answer.

To get a fraction answer, the remainder (3) is put on top of the number doing the dividing ($\frac{3}{6}$). It should then be reduced: $\frac{3}{6} = \frac{1}{2}$, so $6\frac{3}{6} = 6\frac{1}{2}$

To get a decimal answer, the remainder of 3 is carried to the 0 tenths in the tenths column:
$$6.5$$
$$6\overline{)39.0}$$

You could also have just given $6\frac{3}{6}$ as the answer, but 6R3 or 6.3 are wrong, and would not earn you a mark.

If you had used a calculator for: 39 ÷ 6 = , you would have ended up with **6.5**!

19

Every centimetre on the school plan, in question 19 represents 8 m in real life (1 cm : 8 m). For example, 3 cms on the plan represents (3 x 8) 24 m in real life, and 10 cms on the plan represents (10 x 8 m) in real life.
Where the plan measurement is 8.4 cms, this also has to be multiplied by 8 to find the real-life measurement in metres:

$$8.4$$
$$\underline{\times 8}$$
$$67.2$$

20

a) The cost of 12 pupils going to the museum is:
12 x 40 = 480p.
The cost of 1 teacher going to the museum is:
1 x 80p = 80p.
The total therefore, is:
560p, or £5.60 (2 marks).

b) Two marks for expressions such as these:
C = 40 x n + 80
or,
C = 40n + 80
or,
C = 40(n+2).

If your answer was wrong, you will still be given one mark for showing that you had multiplied 40 by n, or, that you had added 80.
For example:
40 x **n** or **n** + 80. So you can see how important it is to show your working!

Test B

18 In a series of 6 maths tests, Jim gained:
7, 8, 3, 5, 6, 10
What is his mean - average - test mark? [6.5]

19 On a plan of the school, the distance from the hall to the staff room, measures 8.4 cms.
If the scale of the plan is 1 centimetre to 8 metres, what is the walking distance - in metres - from the hall to the staff room? [67.2 m]

20 Groups of children have to be accompanied by a teacher to visit the museum. The entry fees are:
Teachers 80p
Pupils 40p

a) How much will it cost 12 pupils and one teacher to visit the museum? Give your answer in pence.

Show your working. You may get a mark.
12 x 40 = 480p
1 x 80 = 80
560

[560 pence]

b) Write a formula for the total cost of a number of pupils and a teacher to visit the museum.
c stands for the total cost of a visit of a teacher and his pupils to the museum. Let **n** be the number of pupils.

[c = 40(n+2)]

page 25, question 20 — **Test B** — **Answers**

21

a) Oven B gets hotter than oven A by **50°**.

If your answer was between 40° and 60°, you will earn a mark.

To **estimate** how much hotter oven B gets than oven A, you should note that oven A's highest temperature (about 160°) **is subtracted** from oven B's highest temperature (about 210°).

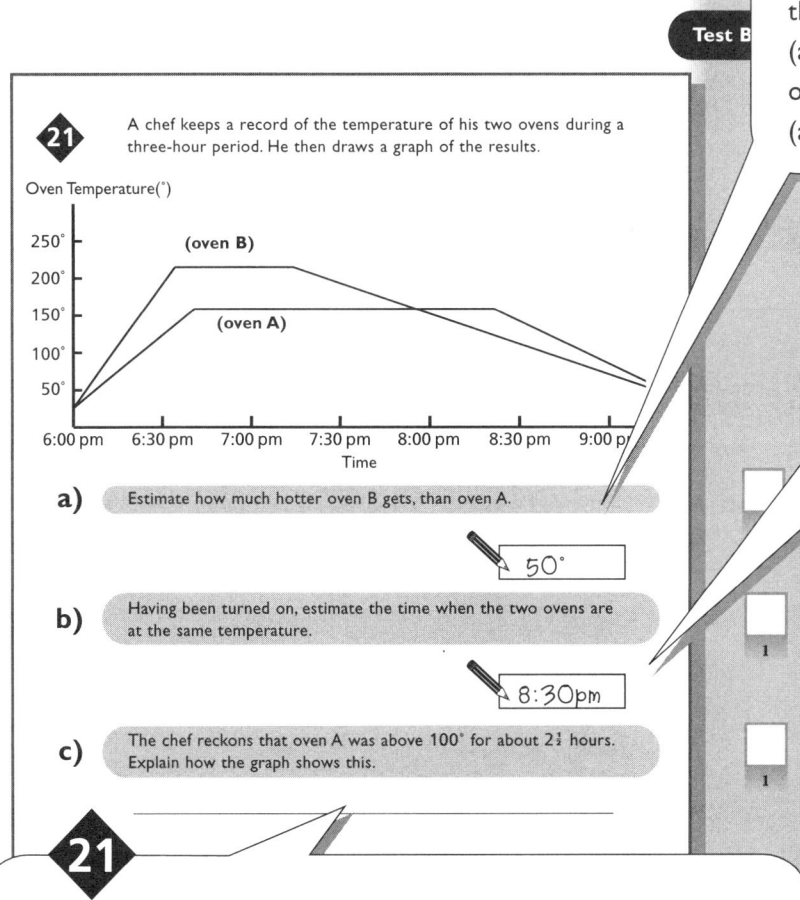

21

21 A chef keeps a record of the temperature of his two ovens during a three-hour period. He then draws a graph of the results.

a) Estimate how much hotter oven B gets, than oven A.

50°

b) Having been turned on, estimate the time when the two ovens are at the same temperature.

8:30pm

c) The chef reckons that oven A was above 100° for about 2½ hours. Explain how the graph shows this.

21

b) The two ovens are at the same temperature **where the two lines of the graph cross** - at about 7:50pm. One mark is allowed for any time between 7:30pm and 8:00pm, but **not** 7:30 and 8:00pm themselves.

If you want to fully understand the graph showing the temperatures of the ovens, you should **follow the pattern of each oven, individually**.

Oven A
◆ Starts off at about 20° (just below halfway between 0° and 50°).
◆ Rises to just over 150° (about 160°).
◆ Remains at that temperature until nearly 8:30pm, when it begins to cool, going down below 100° by about 9:00pm.

Oven B
◆ Starts off at about 20° and rises to just over 200° (about 210°).
◆ Remains there until about 7:15pm (midway between 7:00 pm and 7:30pm).
◆ Temperature then begins to fall, reaching 50° sometime after 9:00pm.

21

c) The oven was above **100°** for about 2½ hours. Your answer should show that you are aware that the **time gap between the points where the 100° level cuts the graph for oven A – between about 6:30pm and about 9:00pm – has been used.**

Your answer might have read like this:
Check when Oven A reaches 100°C and then drops again to 100°C. Work out the time between.

OR

Oven A intersects the graph at 100°, at approximately 6:30pm and then again at approximately 9:00pm, where the line dips below 100° again. If you subtract 6:30 pm from 9:00 pm which is the length of time that the oven has been at that temperature, you will have worked out that the duration was about 2½ hours.

Marks, Scores and Levels

Marking the test

Remember that answers supplied are sample answers. This is especially so in those questions relating to probability. Judge whether an answer has merit and deserves a mark. Consider particularly those questions allocated 2 or more marks, where 1 mark is allocated for working out.

Do not penalise incorrect spelling.

Using the marking grid

Make a note of the marks scored in the tests on the grids below.

Add together the total number of marks awarded for Test A and Test B. Find the level by comparing your child's mark with the corresponding level in the chart below.

Total marks	Level	National comparison for age group
Below 20	has not achieved level 3	Still working towards expected target for age
20 - 40	3	Still working towards national target
41 - 60	4	Achieved national target
61 or above	5	Exceeds national target

TEST A

Question	Marks allocated	Marks scored
1	1	
2	1	
3	1	
4	3	
5	2	
6	1	
7	1	
8	3	
9	2	
10	1	
11	2	
12	3	
13	3	
14	2	
15	5	
16	1	
17	3	
18	2	
19	3	
TOTAL	40	

TEST B

Question	Marks allocated	Marks scored
1	2	
2	1	
3	3	
4	1	
5	1	
6	1	
7	1	
8	4	
9	2	
10	1	
11	2	
12	1	
13	2	
14	2	
15	2	
16	3	
17	2	
18	1	
19	1	
20	4	
21	3	
TOTAL	40	